Collins

KS3
English
Workbook

Paul Burns and Ian Kirby

Revision Tips

Rethink Revision

Have you ever taken part in a quiz and thought '*I know this*!', but no matter how hard you scrabbled around in your brain you just couldn't come up with the answer?

It's very frustrating when this happens, but in a fun situation it doesn't really matter. However, in tests and assessments, it is essential that you can recall the relevant information when you need to.

Most students think that revision is about making sure you **know** *stuff*, but it is also about being confident that you can **retain** that *stuff* over time and **recall** it when needed.

Revision that Really Works

Experts have found that there are two techniques that help with *all* of these things and consistently produce better results in tests and exams compared to other revision techniques.

Applying these techniques to your KS3 revision will ensure you get better results in tests and assessments and will have all the relevant knowledge at your fingertips when you start studying for your GCSEs.

It really isn't rocket science either – you simply need to:
- **test yourself** on each topic as many times as possible
- **leave a gap** between the test sessions.

It is most effective if you leave a good period of time between the test sessions, e.g. between a week and a month. The idea is that just as you start to forget the information, you force yourself to recall it again, keeping it fresh in your mind.

Three Essential Revision Tips

1 **Use Your Time Wisely**
- Allow yourself plenty of time
- Try to start revising six months before tests and assessments – it's more effective and less stressful
- Your revision time is precious so use it wisely – using the techniques described on this page will ensure you revise effectively and efficiently and get the best results
- Don't waste time re-reading the same information over and over again – it's time-consuming and not effective!

2 **Make a Plan**
- Identify all the topics you need to revise (this Workbook will help you)
- Plan at least five sessions for each topic
- A one-hour session should be ample to test yourself on the key ideas for a topic
- Spread out the practice sessions for each topic – the optimum time to leave between each session is about one month but, if this isn't possible, just make the gaps as big as realistically possible.

3 **Test Yourself**
- Methods for testing yourself include: quizzes, practice questions, flashcards, past-papers, explaining a topic to someone else, etc.
- This Workbook gives you opportunities to check your progress
- Don't worry if you get an answer wrong – provided you check what the right answer is, you are more likely to get the same or similar questions right in future!

Visit our website to download your free flashcards, for more information about the benefits of these revision techniques and for further guidance on how to plan ahead and make them work for you.

www.collins.co.uk/collinsks3revision

Contents

ACKNOWLEDGEMENTS

The authors and publisher are grateful to the copyright holders for permission to use quoted materials and images.

All images are ©Shutterstock.com and ©HarperCollins*Publishers*

Every effort has been made to trace copyright holders and obtain their permission for the use of copyright material. The authors and publisher will gladly receive information enabling them to rectify any error or omission in subsequent editions. All facts are correct at time of going to press.

Published by Collins
An imprint of HarperCollins*Publishers*
1 London Bridge Street
London SE1 9GF

ISBN: 978-0-00-839991-7

First published 2020

10 9 8 7 6 5 4 3 2 1

© HarperCollins*Publishers* Ltd. 2020

British Library Cataloguing in Publication Data.

A CIP record of this book is available from the British Library.

Authors: Paul Burns and Ian Kirby
Publisher: Katie Sergeant
Project Manager: Chantal Addy
Editorial: Charlotte Christensen
Cover Design: Kevin Robbins and Sarah Duxbury
Inside Concept Design: Sarah Duxbury, Paul Oates and Ian Wrigley
Text Design and Layout: Jouve India Private Limited
Production: Karen Nulty
Printed in Great Britain by Bell and Bain Ltd, Glasgow

Reading 1

Selecting Key Words and Ideas 1

1 What is meant by the following words/phrases?

a) Key words and ideas

_____ [1]

b) Skim reading

_____ [1]

c) Paraphrasing

_____ [1]

d) Quoting

_____ [1]

Read the passage below and then answer the questions that follow.

Fosbury Hall, beautifully situated in rural Cheshire, was built by the Earl of Fosbury in 1545 but has been altered considerably since then, notably by Sir Henry Morrison, who bought the estate in the 1860s and built two new wings. Sir Henry was one of the wealthiest men in the county, having made a fortune from soap making. His family has also moved away since then, leaving the house and park to the National Trust.

The house has recently been restored so that you can see how Sir Henry, his family and servants lived, as well as admiring his fascinating collection of art and curiosities. There is currently a major tree planting project underway in the grounds.

The house is open every day during the summer. There are organised tours or you can explore on your own. School parties are welcome for special tours and educational 'fun days'.

2 a) Who built Fosbury Hall? _Earl of Fosbury_ [1]

b) Where is the Hall? _In rural Chesire_ [1]

c) When did Sir Henry buy the estate? _The 1860's_ [1]

d) What did Sir Henry collect? _Art and curiosities_ [1]

e) Where are the trees being planted? _In the grounds of Fosbury Hall_ [1]

f) When can people visit the Hall? _Any summer day_ [1]

g) According to the text, why was the house recently restored? _To show everyone_ [1]
how Sir Henry and his family lived there life.

h) How did Sir Henry make his fortune? _He made and sold soap._ [1]

3 Which of the following instructions mean that you must quote directly from the text? Tick **three**.

a) Find and copy a word that shows Sir Henry was rich. ✓

b) Who lived at the Hall in the 1860s? ☐

c) According to the text, what did Sir Henry do as a hobby? ☐

d) Pick out a phrase that tells us when the Hall can be visited. ✓

e) Identify a word or phrase that means 'changed'. ✓ [3]

4 Now answer all the questions in **3**.

a) Wealthy [1]

b) Sir Henry Morrison [1]

c) A Collecting arts & curiosities [1]

d) Any summer day [1]

e) Restored [1]

5 Which of the following phrases are direct quotations from the passage and which are paraphrases? Tick the correct boxes.

		Quotation	Paraphrase
a)	his fascinating collection of art and curiosities		
b)	it's fine to wander about by yourself		
c)	Henry Morrison was very wealthy		
d)	a major tree planting project		
e)	beautifully situated		
f)	the house was built in the sixteenth century		

[6]

6 What is meant by PEE?

P: _____ E: _____ E: _____ [3]

7 Here is an example of the use of PEE. Divide it into its **three** parts. Mark each division with **/**.

The National Trust is busy improving the grounds where a 'major tree planting project is underway'. The word 'major' suggests that there will be a lot of trees planted and 'underway' means that the work is continuing but no indication of when it will be completed is given.

[3]

Read the following passage and answer the questions that follow.

As we sat in that cold village hall in 1939, two things bothered me. One was that I would be separated from Sammy, my little brother; I had promised Mam when she said goodbye to us on the station that I would look after him. The other was that we would be picked last. I was used to being picked last for teams at school because I was always terrible at games, but the people here would not have known that. If they didn't pick us it would be because they just didn't like me, or Sam, or both of us. Because we were too ugly or too scruffy or because there were two of us. Or for any of a thousand reasons that ran through my head while we stood waiting, watching as women came into the village hall, went to the table where a tall, bespectacled, severe lady sat with her list, and then left with a child or two in tow. I tried hard to smile so at least people would think we were friendly.

When the tall, severe lady came over to give us a drink and there were only ten children left (I had been counting them down since the start) she asked me what was worrying me (so much for that friendly smile). I told her that I was worried no-one would pick us. 'Don't be silly,' she replied, 'It doesn't work like that. Chin up!' But she didn't say how it did work.

When there were only seven children remaining, just after someone had left with Annie Rumbold, the naughtiest girl in the school (they'll live to regret that, I thought grimly), I saw a stout, slightly flustered grey-haired woman, looking in our direction while she talked to the tall severe lady. I smiled and nudged Sammy, hissing, 'Look appealing'. The tall lady beckoned us over.

'Here you are, Mrs Bennett,' she said, 'May and Samuel Donovan. Delightful children. Now, you're sure you can manage two?'

'Oh yes,' she replied. 'We want two. George is very keen we have two. So they can be company for each other. Come along, children.' So we picked up our suitcases and our gas masks and followed the stout grey-haired woman out of the village hall. We weren't the last!

Half an hour later, after trudging through mud, clambering over stiles and once falling flat on my face, which caused Mrs Bennett to 'tut tut' and mutter something about unsuitable footwear, we found ourselves outside a massive pair of iron gates between two ancient stone pillars. In the distance, at the end of a long gravel drive was the biggest house I'd ever seen.

'Welcome to Fosbury Hall,' said Mrs Bennett proudly. My jaw dropped.

'Do you live there?' I stuttered.

'Well, not exactly,' she replied.

'Are you a Lady? Are you married to a Lord?'

'Bless you, love, no. I'm married to the gardener. I used to be her Ladyship's maid though, back in the day. But Lady Morrison's long gone. It's full of army folk now, the Hall. Doing war work. All very hush hush.'

8 In what year does the story take place? _____ [1]

9 According to the narrator why was she always the last to be picked for teams?

_____ [1]

10 Pick out **two** words or phrases that describe Mrs Bennett's physical appearance.

_____ [2]

11 Pick out a word or phrase that describes the character of:

a) The woman at the table in the village hall _____ [1]

b) Annie Rumbold _____ [1]

12 Choose **four** statements below which are **true**.

- Shade/tick the boxes of the ones you think are true.
- Choose a maximum of four statements.

a) The narrator of the story is May Donovan.

b) May and Sam are the last to be chosen.

c) The tall woman is May's mother.

d) Mrs Bennett is married to a gardener.

e) May does not want to break the promise she made to her mother.

f) Mrs Bennett owns Fosbury Hall.

g) The Bennetts only wanted to take one child.

h) Fosbury Hall has been taken over by the army. [4]

13 a) Pick a phrase that describes May's reaction to her first sight of Fosbury Hall.

_____ [1]

b) Explain what the phrase means and how it conveys May's feelings.

_____

_____ [2]

Total Marks _____ / 45

Reading 2

Inference, Deduction and Interpretation 1

1 Match the words to their correct definitions.

Infer	To suggest something without directly stating it.
Deduce	To work something out from information you are given.
Interpret	To understand something that is not directly stated.
Imply	To explain the meaning of something.

[4]

2 What can you infer from the following sentences? Choose **two** of the four given answers.

a) Natasha dreams of having a room of her own again.

  i) Natasha has a vivid imagination.

  ii) Natasha shares a room.

  iii) Natasha is lonely.

  iv) Natasha used to have her own room.

[2]

b) Joel scored the only goal of the match in extra time.

  i) Joel's side won the game.

  ii) The score was one all at full time.

  iii) The other team failed to score.

  iv) Joel was the team captain.

[2]

c) The worst thing about living in this flat is that we can't have a dog.

  i) The writer lives in a flat.

  ii) Keeping dogs in a flat is illegal.

  iii) The writer lives alone.

  iv) The writer likes dogs.

[2]

d) Aunt Jemima deposited her dripping umbrella in the hall and strode into the kitchen, leaving a trail of muddy footprints behind her on the hall carpet.

  i) Aunt Jemima has come from outside.

  ii) She is careful and timid.

  iii) It has been raining.

  iv) Aunt Jemima was unprepared for the weather.

[2]

Read the following passage and answer the questions below.

My grandparents have lived in the same house for over fifty years. They moved there when they got married and have been there ever since. It's a three bedroomed terraced house, just off Windy Road. The third bedroom is very small because, according to Gran, it was divided in two not long before they bought the house to make a bathroom. 'Luckily, your Mum was always small,' Grandad jokes, 'so she just about fitted in. But when she got older there was no room for all her clothes. We had to put a wardrobe on the landing; it was a terrible squeeze getting past.' Now the room's full of what Gran calls 'junk'. I used to love rummaging around it, finding the old-fashioned toys that Mum and her brothers, Joe and Mark, used to play with, trying on the old clothes and poring over the photo albums. Next time I go, however, we're going to do a giant clear-out. Gran and Grandad have been watching a lot of antique programmes lately and have got it into their heads that the spare room is what they call 'a little gold mine'.

'We've no antiques as such,' says Gran, 'except for us, but you'd be amazed at what folk'll give for a load of tat nowadays. Vintage, they call it'.

3 **a)** How long have Gran and Grandad been married? _____ [1]

b) Was the house new when they moved in? _____ [1]

c) Was the house built with a bathroom? _____ [1]

d) How many children did Gran and Grandad have? _____ [1]

e) Does the narrator live with her grandparents? _____ [1]

f) Who sleeps in the small bedroom now? _____ [1]

g) What do they mean by saying the room is 'a little gold mine'?

_____ [1]

h) What do Gran and Grandad intend to do with the contents of the small bedroom?

_____ [1]

4 What impression do you get of the narrator's grandparents from the passage? Use quotations from the text to support your answer.

_____
_____
_____ [3]

Reading 2

The following is the beginning of *The Princess*, a short story by DH Lawrence.
Read the extract and answer the questions that follow.

To her father, she was The Princess. To her Boston aunts and uncles she was just Dollie Urquhart, poor little thing.

Colin Urquhart was just a bit mad. He was of an old Scottish family, and he claimed royal blood. The blood of Scottish kings flowed in his veins. On this point, his American relatives said, he was just a bit "off". They could not bear any more to be told which royal blood of Scotland blued his veins. The whole thing was rather ridiculous, and a sore point. The only fact they remembered was that it was not Stuart[1].

He was a handsome man, with a wide-open blue eye that seemed sometimes to be looking at nothing, soft black hair brushed rather low on his low, broad brow, and a very attractive body. Add to this a most beautiful speaking voice, usually rather hushed and diffident, but sometimes resonant and powerful like bronze, and you have the sum of his charms. He looked like some old Celtic hero. He looked as if he should have worn a greyish kilt and a sporran, and shown his knees. His voice came direct out of the hushed Ossianic[2] past.

For the rest, he was one of those gentlemen of sufficient but not excessive means who fifty years ago wandered vaguely about, never arriving anywhere, never doing anything, and never definitely being anything, yet well received in the good society of more than one country.

He did not marry till he was nearly forty, and then it was a wealthy Miss Prescott, from New England. Hannah Prescott at twenty-two was fascinated by the man with the soft black hair not yet touched by grey, and the wide, rather vague blue eyes. Many women had been fascinated before her. But Colin Urquhart, by his very vagueness, had avoided any decisive connection.

Mrs. Urquhart lived three years in the mist and glamour of her husband's presence. And then it broke her. It was like living with a fascinating spectre. About most things he was completely, even ghostly oblivious. He was always charming, courteous, perfectly gracious in that hushed, musical voice of his. But absent. When all came to all, he just wasn't there. "Not all there," as the vulgar say.

He was the father of the little girl she bore at the end of the first year. But this did not substantiate him the more. His very beauty and his haunting musical quality became dreadful to her after the first few months. The strange echo: he was like a living echo! His very flesh, when you touched it, did not seem quite the flesh of a real man.

Perhaps it was that he was a little bit mad. She thought it definitely the night her baby was born.

"Ah, so my little princess has come at last!" he said, in his throaty, singing Celtic voice, like a glad chant, swaying absorbed.

It was a tiny, frail baby, with wide, amazed blue eyes. They christened it Mary Henrietta. She called the little thing My Dollie. He called it always My Princess.

It was useless to fly at him. He just opened his wide blue eyes wider, and took a child-like, silent dignity there was no getting past.

[1] *Stuart* – the surname of the kings and queens of Scotland from 1371 to 1714 and of England from 1603 to 1714.

[2] *Ossianic* – ancient/mythical like the legendary Irish poet Ossian.

5 From the list below circle **four** adjectives that could be used to describe Colin Urquhart.

| romantic | detached | amusing | handsome | lively | conventional | eccentric | angry | [4]

6 According to the text, which of the following statements are **true**? Tick **four**.

a) Colin Urquhart's ancestors were from Scotland. ☐

b) He was related to the Stuart dynasty. ☐

c) People found him attractive. ☐

d) He was ambitious and determined. ☐

e) He had been married before he met Dollie's mother. ☐

f) Mrs Urquhart felt as though she was living with a ghost. ☐

g) She would get very angry with him. ☐

h) Dollie was their first child. ☐ [4]

7 a) What does his use of the word 'princess' tell us about Colin Urquhart's attitude towards his daughter?

_____

_____ [2]

b) What does the phrase 'poor little thing' tell us about the aunts and uncles' attitude?

_____ [1]

c) What do you think Colin's relatives mean by his being 'off'?

_____ [1]

8 How do Hannah's feelings about her husband change? Support your answer with close reference to the text. Write your answer on a separate piece of paper. [8]

Total Marks _____ / 45

Reading 3

How Ideas are Organised 1

1 Match these words/phrases to their correct definitions.

Paragraph	A section of a poem, sometimes referred to as a 'verse'.
Stanza	Ordering events by time, from first to last.
Chronological order	A section of a piece of prose.
Flashback	Ending a text by returning to or referring back to the beginning.
Circular structure	Describing or narrating something that happened before the main action.

[5]

2 Give **four** reasons for starting a new paragraph.

....

.... [4]

3 Here are a list of historical events:

- Norman Conquest 1066
- Second World War 1939–1945
- Waterloo 1815
- Agincourt 1415
- First World War 1914–1918

Place the events in...

a) alphabetical order. ....

.... [1]

b) chronological order. ....

.... [1]

c) reverse chronological order. ....

.... [1]

4 Read the following passage and then match the descriptions below to each paragraph. Write the correct paragraph numbers in the boxes.

1   I usually find school trips extremely boring, except of course the one to a theme park at the end of term. However, last year's history trip was an experience I'll never forget.

2 We went to a castle that was built in the middle ages. I don't know exactly when because I've lost all the notes we were given. There was a lot of stuff about moats and drawbridges and various kings and who they were fighting against. If you want to know you can look it up.

3 It wasn't all that stuff that made the trip memorable, although I have to admit the jousting was pretty impressive and the falconry demonstration wasn't too bad. It was what Sammy did.

4 Before we go on, I'd better tell you about Sammy. Sammy has been my best mate since primary school. We live in the same street, we've always sat together in class and the teachers are always getting us mixed up. I say he 'has been' my friend but after what he did that day, I'm not so sure.

a) The writer gives more information about the trip but suggests that the place itself was of little interest. ☐ [1]

b) The writer gives some background on Sammy and their relationship before returning to the subject of the trip. ☐ [1]

c) The writer introduces the subject of the passage, a school trip, and suggests that something interesting happened. ☐ [1]

d) The writer returns to the idea that the trip was memorable and shifts focus to Sammy, creating interest in the reader. ☐ [1]

5 Here are six words and phrases that are often used as connectives or discourse markers. Insert them in the passage below so that it makes sense.

However	Despite	The next day	Because of	So	Basically

_____ Sammy's best efforts, we all got back to school safely. _____ , that was not the end of the story. _____ we were all summoned to something called a 'special assembly'. _____ it was the headteacher ranting on about good behaviour, health and safety, the school's reputation and all the usual stuff.

_____ what had gone on, we were told that we wouldn't be allowed on any more trips for the rest of the year. Some of the others were really upset and, of course, they all blamed Sammy. I was pleased. I hated school trips. _____ I decided to stay friends with Sammy after all. [6]

Reading 3

How Ideas are Organised 2

This is an article from a school website. Read it and answer the questions that follow.

YOUR FUTURE – YOUR CHOICE

At the end of Year 9 you will have to choose your GCSE subjects. Here are some tips on how to do it.

What are options and why do we have them?

Options are choices. For GCSE some subjects are not optional: everybody has to take English, Mathematics and Science. In Science you can either take a combined course or three separate sciences (Physics, Chemistry and Biology). You will also continue with IT, Citizenship and PE. You do not have to sit exams in these subjects, although you can opt to take IT or PE for GCSE.

Overall, you will be studying fewer subjects than you do now. This is because the demands of the GCSE curriculum mean that you need to spend a lot more time on each subject in order to reach the required standard.

How many options can I choose?

If you have decided to do separate sciences, you should choose three additional subjects. If not, you should choose four.

What subjects are available?

At Lark Vale Academy we have a wide range of subjects to choose from. Look at the table below. You must choose at least one subject from the first column. Click on the links to find out more about each subject:

EBacc subjects	Other subjects	
• French	• Art	• PE
• Geography	• Business Studies	• Religious Studies
• German	• Computer Science	
• History	• Drama	
• Spanish	• Food and Nutrition	

How do I choose?

There are a number of things you should take into account when choosing your options. Among them are:

- Enjoyment – you're going to spend two years studying the subject so it is really important that you enjoy it.
- Achievement – which subjects do you think you are good at? By now you should have a clear idea about which subjects you shine at and which are a struggle.
- Careers – it may seem like a long way off, but your choices are relevant to your career. For example, if you want to be a doctor, it is a good idea to get a thorough grounding in sciences. If you are thinking of working abroad, modern languages would be a good choice.
- Balance – think of your timetable as a whole. Variety is the spice of life and you might get more out of life if you choose some practical subjects, such as Food and Nutrition or PE, and some that are more academic. And don't forget the enrichment that can come from subjects such as Art and Drama.

What If I need help choosing?

There's plenty of help available. Talk to your parents and your teachers. Read the **options booklet** that you have been given and/or follow the subject links on this page. And don't forget to come to the **Options Fair** at Lark Vale on 5th March.

6 **a)** Identify and copy out:

    i) the headline _____ [1]

    ii) the strapline

_____ [1]

  b) What is the purpose of the strapline?

_____

_____ [2]

  c) How do the subheadings help readers?

_____

_____ [2]

7 The writer makes use of bullet points in two different sections of the text. What are they used for?

_____

_____ [2]

8 Why do you think the subheadings are in the form of questions?

_____

_____ [2]

9 In your own words, briefly summarise the contents of each of the sections. The first one has been done for you.

Subheading	Content
What are options and why do we have them?	The writer explains what is meant by 'options' and why students have to make a choice.
How many options can I choose?	a)
What subjects are available?	b)
How do I choose?	c)
What if I need help choosing?	d)

[8]

Total Marks _____ / 40

Reading 4

Exploring Language Choices 1

1 Below are four synonyms for 'speak'. Briefly explain the precise meaning of each:

a) mumble _____ [1]

b) whisper _____ [1]

c) chatter _____ [1]

d) harangue _____ [1]

2 Here are some examples of the use of literary techniques. State which of them contains:

- a metaphor
- a simile
- alliteration
- assonance
- onomatopoeia
- personification.

a) Fear gripped us all. _____ [1]

b) Zara entered like a whirlwind. _____ [1]

c) The door shut behind her with a mighty clang. _____ [1]

d) 'It's wild, wet and windy out there,' she exclaimed. _____ [1]

e) She was so frozen and cold. _____ [1]

f) 'You're pure gold', he said. _____ [1]

3 Explain the effect of the similes used in the quotations below. The first one has been done for you.

O my Luve's like the melodie That's sweetly play'd in tune. (Robert Burns)	By comparing his love to a melody 'play'd in tune' the poet suggests that she is beautiful and without imperfections.
What passing bell for these who die as cattle? (Wilfred Owen)	**a)**
I wander'd lonely as a cloud (William Wordsworth)	**b)**

[4]

4 Insert the correct word or phrase from the box into the following sentences.

ellipsis	non-standard English	exclamation mark	first person
	second person	present tense	imperatives

a) _____ are used to give the reader instructions or advice. [1]

b) Writers can use _____ to show a thought trailing off, make the reader wonder what will happen next or to show that some words have been omitted. [1]

c) Sometimes a writer will use an _____ to show excitement or surprise. They should be used sparingly. [1]

d) The use of the _____ can make a story seem more immediate and vivid, as if it is happening now. [1]

e) _____ includes dialect and slang. It creates an informal tone. [1]

f) The use of both the _____ (I/we) and the _____ (you) can make a text more personal, involving the reader. [2]

5 State the rhetorical devices used in the following examples.

a) The parish council is responsible for our inadequate street lighting, the pot holes in our roads and the disgraceful state of the recreation ground.

_____ [1]

b) Our daily lives have been ruined by pot holes the size of craters.

_____ [1]

c) And who must take ultimate responsibility for this chaos?

_____ [1]

6 Explain how, in each of the sentences in question **5**, the writer uses rhetoric to influence the reader or listener.

a) _____

_____ [2]

b) _____

_____ [2]

c) _____

_____ [2]

Exploring Language Choices 2

Read the poem below and answer the questions that follow.

In this poem, Hardy describes a meeting at a railway station between a boy and a convict, who is guarded by a police officer.

At the Railway Station, Upway

by Thomas Hardy

'There is not much that I can do,
For I've no money that's quite my own!'
Spoke up the pitying child–
A little boy with a violin

5   At the station before the train came in,–
'But I can play my fiddle to you,
And a nice one 'tis, and good in tone!'

The man in the handcuffs smiled;
The constable looked, and he smiled too,

10 As the fiddle began to twang;
And the man in the handcuffs suddenly sang
With grimful glee:
'This life so free
Is the thing for me!'

15 And the constable smiled, and said no word,
As if unconscious of what he heard;
And so they went on till the train came in--
The convict, and boy with the violin.

7 **a)** Who is speaking in the first two lines of the poem? Tick **one**.

The poet ☐

The boy ☐

The convict ☐

The constable ☐   [1]

b) How does the poet show that these are not his words but those of a character in the poem?

_____   [1]

8 In the first stanza the poet uses two different nouns for the same thing: 'violin' and 'fiddle'. Explain why he uses 'fiddle' rather than 'violin' in line 6.

....

.... [2]

9 **a)** From the first stanza pick an adjective that describes the boy's attitude to the prisoner.

.... [1]

b) From the second stanza pick a verb that is repeated to convey the mood of the meeting.

.... [1]

10 Explain how the phrase, 'the man in the handcuffs' affects the reader's interpretation of what is happening in the poem.

....

....

....

.... [4]

11 The song that the prisoner sings could be described as 'ironic'. Explain why.

....

.... [2]

12 In line 12 the poet uses an oxymoron, 'grimful glee' to describe the way in which the convict sings.

a) Explain what is meant by an 'oxymoron'.

.... [1]

b) Explain the effect of the poet's use of this phrase on the reader.

....

.... [2]

13 How does Hardy use language in the second stanza to convey the mood on the railway platform?

....

....

....

.... [5]

Total Marks .... / 50

Reading 5

1 What do you think is the **primary** purpose of the following sentences? Choose from the words in the box:

| describe | inform | instruct | advise | argue | persuade | entertain |

  a) A school web page that gives details of all the school staff. .... [1]

  b) A poster asking you to donate money to a charity. .... [1]

  c) A leaflet about how to assemble a chest of drawers. .... [1]

  d) A nonsense poem. .... [1]

  e) A poem about the sunset. .... [1]

  f) A series of comments on a blog, giving the writers' views. .... [1]

  g) A booklet about ways to stay healthy and avoid illness. .... [1]

2 Identify the three **imperatives** in the following instruction.

> After you have heated the oil, chop the onions finely. Then place them in the pan and fry them gently.

.... [3]

3 When writing to argue, persuade or advise, writers often use **modal verbs**. For each of the following sentences identify the modal verb and the purpose of the text.

  a) You should not give in to pressure from your peers.

  Modal verb ....

  Purpose of text .... [2]

  b) I firmly believe that the abolition of homework would improve learning.

  Modal verb ....

  Purpose of text .... [2]

  c) You may wish to give a larger amount and so help more people.

  Modal verb ....

  Purpose of text .... [2]

4 Write a sentence or two explaining the purposes of each of the following passages. Each one has two purposes. The first one has been done for you.

At this time of year it is important that you should think about getting your flu jab. You can come into the surgery any time between 8 a.m. and 6 p.m. Monday to Friday.	*The writer **advises** readers to get a flu jab and **informs** them of when they can get one.*
I strongly object to the proposed changes in the timetable. May I suggest that you look at them again and invite students to give their views?	**a)**
Continue along the coastal path for a mile before taking the turning on the left and walking to the top of the hill. The view of the island's whitewashed buildings glimmering in the sun, glimpsed across the azure sea, is well worth the climb.	**b)**

[4]

5 Look again at the three passages in question **4**. Identify each writer's point of view and explain how he/she uses language to convey that point of view.

a) ....
....
....
[3]

b) ....
....
....
[3]

c) ....
....
....
[3]

6 Now briefly explain what effect each of the paragraphs in question **4** has on you, the reader.

a) ....
....
[1]

b) ....
....
[1]

c) ....
....
[1]

Explaining Purposes and Viewpoints 2

Read the text below, taken from a speech given at a school prize-giving, and answer the questions that follow.

It is a great honour for me to be asked to give out the prizes at my old school and it has been a wonderful experience looking around, seeing what has changed and what has stayed the same over the last twenty years. Most of all, I have enjoyed meeting all of you.

I am not going to talk about my achievements and how I got where I am today. If you want to know more, you can always look it up on the internet – but not right away, please! I want to speak to you today about what it was like for me growing up around here and about someone who has inspired me.

Don't worry. I'm not going to give you one of those sob stories about how difficult life was and how I struggled to overcome the odds. If there is one thing I don't like hearing it is politicians and celebrities banging on about their awful lives and how unfortunate they were compared to others. It's victim culture at its worst. I won't name names but, quite frankly, if you look into their backgrounds, most of their claims don't really stack up anyway.

I had a very happy childhood. We had our problems at times but we were fed and clothed, we were comfortable and, most importantly, we knew we were loved. As a little girl, I had a wonderful role model in my Gran. My Gran was born and brought up just a few streets from here. When she was growing up in the nineteen thirties life really was hard. Most people struggled to get by but they stuck together and, as Gran said, 'just got on with it'. They also 'just got on with it' when the war came and their lives were in constant danger, carrying on despite the dropping bombs. Gran was working nights at the munitions factory when a bomb dropped on her street, killing the family next door. Everyone lost loved ones. But they 'just got on with it'.

In spite of these experiences, or maybe because of them, she was one of the most cheerful and optimistic people you could ever hope to meet. She taught us to cook. She took us on long walks, teaching us about nature. She entertained us by singing old songs and dancing around the kitchen. If we were sick or upset, she made us feel better. She helped to give us a secure childhood and a good start in life. She wasn't an academic or a politician or a movie star, but she was a good, caring woman. That's the kind of person I aspire to be and it's the kind of person I hope many of you will be. Don't dwell on any problems or disadvantages you might encounter. Look on the bright side, do your best and just get on with it.

7 Pick out a sentence from the first paragraph that is designed to flatter the audience.

[1]

8 Which **three** of the following statements describe the speaker's purposes?

   a) To describe her grandmother. ☐

   b) To persuade the audience to study history. ☐

   c) To explain what she does for a living. ☐

   d) To advise her audience about how to have a happy life. ☐

   e) To argue against what she sees as 'victim culture'. ☐

   f) To inform them about their options when they leave school. ☐ [3]

9 Pick out **two** phrases from the second paragraph that imply the speaker is a very successful

person. ....

.... [2]

10 Explain what is meant by the following phrases and what they tell us about the speaker's views.
Write your answer on a separate piece of paper if needed.

Phrase	Explanation	The writer's view
'victim culture'	a)	b)
'their claims don't really stack up'	c)	d)
'a wonderful role model'	e)	f)

[6]

11 Look again at the last two paragraphs.

   a) Explain why the speaker considers her grandmother to be a good role model.

   ....

   ....

   .... [3]

   b) How does the speaker use language to convey her grandmother's character?

   ....

   ....

   .... [3]

Total Marks .... / 47

Reading 6

Structuring a Longer Response 1

1 If the question asks, for example, 'how does the writer use language to describe the mountains', which **five** of the following aspects of the text could you comment on?

a) The writer's use of imagery. ☐

b) The way sentences are structured. ☐

c) How the extract relates to the passage as a whole. ☐

d) Your opinion about the mountains. ☐

e) The writer's use of rhetorical techniques. ☐

f) The type of narrator used. ☐

g) What you know about the writer. ☐

h) The writer's choice of vocabulary. ☐

[5]

2 If a question asks how a writer has structured a text there may be bullet points suggesting you write about:

- how or why the writer changes the focus
- any other structural features.

a) Explain what is meant by **changing focus**.

....

....

.... [3]

b) Give **three** examples of structural features a writer might use to interest the reader.

.... [3]

3 Here is an extract from *The Wind in The Willows* by Kenneth Grahame. Read it and answer the question below. In this extract, Mole becomes nervous after setting out to explore the wild wood on his own.

Try to spend no more than ten minutes answering the question. Use between one and one and a half sheets of A4 paper.

He quickened his pace, telling himself cheerfully not to begin imaging things, or there would be simply no end to it. He passed another hole, and another, and another; and then – yes! – no! – yes! Certainly a little narrow face, with hard eyes, had flashed for an instant from a hole, and was gone. He hesitated – braced himself for an effort and strode on. Then suddenly, and as if it had been so all the time, every hole, far and near, and there were hundreds of them, seemed to possess its face, coming and going rapidly, all firing on him evil glances of malice: all hard-eyed and evil and sharp.

How does the writer use language here to describe Mole's experience and his feelings?

You could include the writer's use of:

- words and phrases
- language features and techniques
- sentence forms. [8]

4 Read the **two** texts below and answer the question that follows.

Spend no more than ten minutes on this question and use no more than two sheets of A4 paper. Try to find at least **four** differences between the texts.

Source A

The Silver Sea

To the young, of course, the sea appeals with a force which we have all experienced, but which gradually vanishes with the flight of years. Yet it never entirely leaves us, and however old we may be there are but few inlanders for whom the seaside with its refreshing breezes, to say nothing of its childhood memories, has not some charm. The Redcar beach has been described as "The Children's Paradise", and anyone who has watched the happy countenances of the rising generation, as they play among the sand, making castles, pies, miniature lakes, and other forms of amusement so dear to the youthful heart, must admit that there is much justification for the title. At Eastertide, if fine weather prevails, we may look for thousands of little ones sporting themselves on the beautiful golden strand – the finest on the North-East Coast.

(from *The Daily Gazette for Middlesbrough,* 14 April 1908)

Source B

The beach that day was almost deserted. Hardly surprising – it was a miserable day, cold, wet and windy. Certainly nobody was sunbathing. There were a few random groups of people sheltering close to the sand dunes. Here, an elderly couple, sitting on striped picnic chairs, wrapped up in scarves and anoraks, serenely munching their way through a selection of sandwiches and pastries which they had brought in plastic boxes. They hardly spoke but they seemed happy enough. There, a family group of man, woman and two children aged perhaps six and eight, protected by a garish wind break, each sitting a little way from the other absorbed by their phones, barely raising their heads to look at the sea. Out of the sea emerged a cheerful but shivering woman in a navy-blue swimsuit, fresh from her morning dip. She shouted a hearty greeting as I passed with Henry, my Labrador. He recognized a kindred spirit and rushed over to return the greeting by jumping up and licking her enthusiastically.

(Dan Featherstone, 2020)

Use details from both sources.

Write a summary of the differences between the two writers' experiences of the beach. [8]

Reading 6

Structuring a Longer Response 2

Read the extract below from *A Child's History of England* by
Charles Dickens and answer the questions that follow.

As great and good in peace, as he was great and good in war, KING ALFRED
never rested from his labours to improve his people. He loved to talk with clever
men, and with travellers from foreign countries, and to write down what they told
him, for his people to read. He had studied Latin after learning to read English, and
5 now another of his labours was, to translate Latin books into the English-Saxon
tongue, that his people might be interested, and improved by their contents.
He made just laws, that they might live more happily and freely; he turned away all
partial judges, that no wrong might be done them; he was so careful of their property,
and punished robbers so severely, that it was a common thing to say that under the
10 great KING ALFRED, garlands of golden chains and jewels might have hung across the
streets, and no man would have touched one. He founded schools; he patiently heard
causes himself in his Court of Justice; the great desires of his heart were, to do right to
all his subjects, and to leave England better, wiser, happier in all ways, than he found
it. His industry in these efforts was quite astonishing. Every day he divided into certain
15 portions, and in each portion devoted himself to a certain pursuit. That he might divide
his time exactly, he had wax torches or candles made, which were all of the same size,
were notched across at regular distances, and were always kept burning. Thus, as the
candles burnt down, he divided the day into notches, almost as accurately as we now
divide it into hours upon the clock. But when the candles were first invented, it was
20 found that the wind and draughts of air, blowing into the palace through the doors
and windows, and through the chinks in the walls, caused them to gutter and burn
unequally. To prevent this, the King had them put into cases formed of wood and white
horn. And these were the first lanthorns[1] ever made in England.

All this time, he was afflicted with a terrible unknown disease, which caused him
25 violent and frequent pain that nothing could relieve. He bore it, as he had borne all the
troubles of his life, like a brave good man, until he was fifty-three years old; and then,
having reigned thirty years, he died. He died in the year nine hundred and one; but,
long ago as that is, his fame, and the love and gratitude with which his subjects regarded
him, are freshly remembered to the present hour.

[1] *Lanthorn* – an old spelling of 'lantern'

5 This question asks for your reaction to a statement. You should think about what impressions you form from reading the text about what the writer is describing and how he uses language to create these impressions. Write your answers on a separate piece of paper.

> A reader has said, 'In this extract Dickens successfully manages to make King Alfred appear both heroic and human'.
>
> To what extent do you agree with that statement?
>
> In your response you should:
>
> - write about your own impressions of King Alfred
> - evaluate how the writer has created these impressions
> - support your opinions with quotations from the text.

First, make some notes about the first bullet point. Quickly jot down the impressions you get about King Alfred from the text and pick out short quotations to support your points. Try to make at least **four** separate points.

My impressions of King Alfred	Supporting quotation(s)

Now consider the second bullet point and make brief notes. Focus on the language the writer used, for example choice of vocabulary and sentence structure. Pick out some appropriate short quotations to support each point. Try to make at least **four** separate points.

How Dickens creates these impressions	Supporting quotation(s)

Using your notes, answer the question. Spend about twenty minutes on your answer, using no more than three pages.

[20]

Total Marks _____ / 47

Progress Test 1

Read this extract from *The Secret Garden* by Frances Hodgson Burnett, first published in 1911, and answer the questions that follow. In the extract, Mary has just arrived in England from India and is being taken by carriage to her new home on the moors.

"What is a moor?" she said suddenly to Mrs. Medlock.

"Look out of the window in about ten minutes and you'll see," the woman answered. "We've got to drive five miles across Missel Moor before we get to the Manor. You won't see much because it's a dark night, but you can see something."

Mary asked no more questions but waited in the darkness of her corner, keeping her eyes on the window. The carriage lamps cast rays of light a little distance ahead of them and she caught glimpses of the things they passed. After they had left the station they had driven through a tiny village and she had seen whitewashed cottages and the lights of a public house. Then they had passed a church and a vicarage and a little shop-window or so in a cottage with toys and sweets and odd things set out for sale. Then they were on the highroad and she saw hedges and trees. After that there seemed nothing different for a long time – or at least it seemed a long time to her.

At last the horses began to go more slowly, as if they were climbing up-hill, and presently there seemed to be no more hedges and no more trees. She could see nothing, in fact, but a dense darkness on either side. She leaned forward and pressed her face against the window just as the carriage gave a big jolt.

"Eh! We're on the moor now sure enough," said Mrs. Medlock.

1 List **four** things that Mary sees from the carriage.

_____   _____

_____   _____ [4]

2 How does the writer give a sense of how isolated the Manor is? Refer to the text in your answer.

_____

_____

_____

_____ [4]

3 Briefly state the focus of each paragraph. The first one has been done for you.

1. From 'What is a moor?...'	The focus is on Mary and her desire to find out about the moor.
2. From 'Look out of the window...'	a)
3. From 'Mary asked no more questions...'	b)
4. 'At last the horses...'	c)
5. From 'Eh! We're on the moor...'	d)

[4]

Now read this poem by Christina Rossetti (1830–1894) and answer the questions that follow.

The Wind by *Christina Rossetti*

Who has seen the wind?
Neither I nor you;
But when the leaves hang trembling
The wind is passing through.

Who has seen the wind?
Neither you nor I;
But when the trees bow down their heads
The wind is passing by.

4 Explain how the poem is structured in terms of:

a) stanzas and lines

[1]

b) rhyme

[1]

c) rhythm/metre

[1]

5 Give an example from the text of a rhetorical question and explain the effect of its use.

[2]

6 Give an example from the text of personification and comment on its effect.

[2]

7 What do you think the poet is using the wind as a metaphor for? Support your answer with evidence from the text.

[4]

Now read this extract from an article published in *The Times* in 1920.

Source A

Summer Excursions

There are signs of a possible repetition of last year's clamour for cheap excursion trains during the summer holiday season, so it is desirable to explain the situation before any such agitation can develop. The Ministry of Transport, which does not wish to incur additional unpopularity, was anxious that excursion trains should be run if possible, but the difficulties are likely to be too great. The Ministry has informed a deputation of London members that no excursions can be provided at Easter or Whitsuntide, and the public had better make up their minds that little will be done during the summer months. The utmost that can be expected is the provision of a few special trains at the old ordinary fares. Several factors have made the refusal necessary. One is that (probably owing to higher wages) far more people are using the railways, in spite of the increased fares, than before the war, while the number of season-ticket holders has risen by 50 per cent. No British railway has yet been able to restore its normal pre-war service of passenger trains, and we are still about 25 per cent below the pre-war standard. But the main cause is the lack of locomotives.

8 Which **three** of these statements describe the purpose of the text?

a) To inform readers that there will be no cheap trains laid on for excursions. ☐

b) To persuade readers to take the train. ☐

c) To argue the case for lower fares. ☐

d) To criticize the government's actions. ☐

e) To defend the government's policy. ☐

f) To explain the reasons for the Ministry's refusal to put on extra trains. ☐ [3]

9 Find and copy an example of the use of:

a) a subordinate clause introduced by a relative pronoun

.... [1]

b) parenthesis

.... [1]

c) a simple sentence

.... [1]

Now read this contemporary piece on a similar subject.

Source B

Happy Days Are Here Again!

Happy Days Travel, Britain's leading specialist coach tour company, are pleased and excited to announce our new programme for the coming year. This year, owing to popular demand and the increasing popularity of the 'staycation', we are running more trips than ever. There will be trips from all major towns and cities to the seaside, to beautiful rural towns and villages, and to major historical and cultural attractions. Our trips will run throughout the year, with extra services laid on at times of peak demand such as Easter and the May bank holidays. What's more, thanks to increased capacity and efficiency, we can guarantee we will keep our prices low.

10 Look again at Source A: 'Summer Excursions'. Write a summary of the differences between the plans described in that piece and the plans described in Source B: 'Happy Days Are Here Again!' Use details from both texts in your answer.

Write your answer on a separate piece of paper. [8]

Total Marks .... / 37

Writing 1

Purpose, Audience and Form

1 What would be the purpose, audience and form of the following **four** tasks?

a) You have been interviewing people about a new leisure development in your area. Write an article for your local newspaper informing readers about people's different views.

Purpose: ....

Audience: ....

Form: .... **[3]**

b) You want to run a charity evening at your local school to raise money for a children's charity. Write a speech to be presented in front of the school governors, persuading them to let you organise the event.

Purpose: ....

Audience: ....

Form: .... **[3]**

c) You've noticed that other students at your school are making no attempt to reuse and recycle. Write the text for a leaflet that will be handed out to all students, explaining five ways in which they can change their behaviour in order to help the environment.

Purpose: ....

Audience: ....

Form: .... **[3]**

d) A national newspaper is running a writing competition to present both sides of an argument. The topic is 'The UK Press Is Guilty Of Bullying Celebrities'. The winning article will be published in the newspaper.

Purpose: ....

Audience: ....

Form: .... **[3]**

2 Summarise some of the differences between an article and a speech.

_____

_____

_____

_____

_____

_____ [4]

3 Summarise some of the similarities and differences between how to address a teenage audience and an adult audience.

_____

_____

_____

_____

_____

_____ [4]

4 Choose **one** of the four writing tasks from question **1**. Write your opening paragraph. Make sure to use language and structure that clearly establishes the purpose, audience, and form of your response.

_____

_____

_____

_____

_____

_____ [4]

Total Marks _____ / 24

Writing 2

Paragraphs and Connectives

1 Changes in what **three** things are often accompanied by a new paragraph?

....

.... [3]

2 Break the text below into four paragraphs using // to signal where the three new paragraphs should begin.

The house on Main Street was hundreds of years old. Everyone had seen it and talked about it but few had ever been inside. The few that had entered the house had never returned. It was midnight when Cathy climbed the rusty gates to enter the grounds. The trees swayed violently as the wind howled. The moon shone eerily across the overgrown garden, its ghostly light interrupting the drifting shadows. When she reached the front door, she was surprised to find it unlocked. The door creaked open with the noise of bones shattering. A dank, stale smell crept from the house and seemed to envelop her. Stepping inside she saw that everything was draped in a thick curtain of dust and cobwebs. Spiders crawled slowly across the walls and she could hear something small, probably mice, scuttling behind the walls.

[3]

3 Continue Cathy's exploration of the house, using a new paragraph whenever appropriate.

....

....

....

....

....

....

....

....

....

....

[3]

4 Write down **three** connectives for each of the following categories:

a) time

_____

b) sequence

_____

c) cause and effect

_____

d) compare

_____

e) contrast

_____

f) development

_____ [18]

5 Read the sentences below. Each one is missing a connective. Decide what category of connective needs to be used and select a specific word.

a) To begin making the cake, weigh out 250g of butter and cream it with a fork. _____ add 250g of caster sugar and blend with the sugar.

Category: _____

b) Katie is five years old and enjoys drawing. _____ her brother, Max, is seven and most enjoys riding his bike.

Category: _____

c) The man lifted the bubbling saucepan from the hob, crying out in pain _____ the extreme heat of the handle.

Category: _____

d) A healthy diet is quite easy to maintain. _____ it is a tasty alternative to junk food.

Category: _____ [8]

Total Marks _____ / 35

Writing 3

1 Decide whether the following sentences are simple, compound or complex.

a) The house was blue.

_____ [1]

b) Turning towards the camera, the girl gave a big smile.

_____ [1]

c) The cheese was mouldy and it was beginning to smell.

_____ [1]

d) It was a beautiful day but the boy had to stay indoors.

_____ [1]

e) The cold fog drifted between the trees.

_____ [1]

f) The street, usually so quiet, was packed with people.

_____ [1]

2 Rewrite the sentences below by moving the subordinate clause to a different position.

a) The cake began to rise, gradually turning to a golden brown colour.

_____ [1]

b) The armchair, although old and threadbare, was incredibly comfortable.

_____ [1]

c) Looking nervously at the clock, the boy wrote hurriedly to finish the exam.

_____ [1]

3 Turn the following simple sentences into complex sentences by adding a subordinate clause. Your subordinate clause can go before, after, or in the middle of your main clause.

a) The girls danced.

_____ [1]

b) The boy found the fridge was empty.

_____ [1]

c) Four cars raced down the road.

_____ [1]

4 Write the following **four** verbs in the present, past, future and conditional tenses, using the first person.

a) to go ....

.... [4]

b) to listen ....

.... [4]

c) to make ....

.... [4]

d) to catch ....

.... [4]

5 Rewrite these sentences in the past tense. There are **five** errors.

It is Thursday and I am going to my friend's house. On the way, I buy some chocolate and a bottle of apple juice. The sun is shining and I feel in a really good mood.

....

....

.... [5]

6 Rewrite these sentences so they are grammatically correct. Use the past tense and the first person. There are **12** errors.

I goed to school yesterday, but there is no one there. I would have walked around for quite a while, calling out to trying and getting someone's attention. I looked through the windows, and there is no one in any of the classes. It would be scary being all alone in such a familiar place. Suddenly with great embarrassment I realise that it were Saturday.

....

....

....

....

.... [12]

Total Marks .... / 45

Writing 4

1 When are the **two** occasions that you need to use an apostrophe?

.... [2]

2 Add the correct apostrophes to these sentences.

a) The dogs bowl was empty.

b) I couldnt find the exit.

c) If theyre going then so am I.

d) Joes shirt was ripped.

e) The three girls clothes were covered in mud.

f) Ive got a headache. [6]

3 Add the correct commas to these sentences.

a) Covered with a thick layer of cobwebs the windows were impossible to see through.

b) The roof, due to several missing tiles let in water whenever it rained.

c) The cupboards were full of jars bottles cans and tins.

d) The wooden door was old and cracked paint peeling from its rough surface. [4]

4 Correct the punctuation in the sentences below. There are **eight** errors.

Harry followed his dogs paw prints through the snow wondering what he would find. As he reached a tall tree he saw his brothers shoe lying on the ground. Picking it up Harry noticed blood on the shoes leather. He dropped it in horror. The forest full of shadows and strange sounds seemed to close around him. [8]

5 Write the plural forms of the following words.

a) cat ....

b) mouse ....

c) activity ....

d) box ....

e) child ....

f) tooth ....

g) shelf .... [7]

6 Find and correct the spelling mistake in each of these sentences.

a) The horses were taken to the stabel.

b) Looking for some attenshun, the boy shouted and screamed.

c) After the party, the kitchen looked horrendus.

d) The plate smashed to peices.

e) The man through the ball to his son.

f) She brought six bars of chocolate from the shop.

g) He asked her to weight by the door.

h) The king had come to the end of his rain.

i) The girls loved to go swiming.

j) She slamed the window shut.

k) A little happyness goes a long way.

l) The woman had spent all her saveings. [12]

7 Rewrite these sentences so they contain correct punctuation and spelling. There are **22** errors.

Lucys room was a mess. There were clothes magazines toys and ornaments covering the floor. Looking around her she didnt know wear to start. She realised, starring at the overflowing cuboards and draws that she simply had to many things. She picked up an old pear of jeans considdering if she still needed them. Then she gatherd up some discarded bookes and began to flick threw them. She looked agen at the chaos surounding her. 'Wood it be so bad just to leave it' she wondered.

[22]

Total Marks / 61

Writing 5

Read this sample writing task and answer the questions that follow.

> As part of a national competition, write the text for a leaflet persuading parents to adopt a vegetarian lifestyle for their family.

1 Identify the purpose, audience and form.

Purpose: .... Audience: ....

Form: .... [3]

2 Spend a few minutes mindmapping the idea of a vegetarian lifestyle. Think about its possible benefits to individuals and the world; you might also consider any arguments against vegetarianism that you could try to counter. [6]

A vegetarian lifestyle

3 Now complete the plan that has been started for you. Think about what you will write about and any specific techniques that you could include to match your purpose. Complete your answer on a separate piece of paper.

Structure	Techniques
Introduction: *Summarise paragraph content*	*Second person*
Paragraph 1: *Why vegetarianism is healthier for families. Vitamins, meat linked to heart disease, 5-a-day, natural / organic.*	*Lists and emotive language*
Paragraph 2:	
Paragraph 3:	
Paragraph 4:	
Paragraph 5:	

[8]

4 Imagine you are completing the task in exam conditions. Start by writing an introduction that summarises the different aspects of the topic that your leaflet will include. It should be fairly brief so aim for 2–3 sentences.

....

....

....

....

[3]

5 The first paragraph has been started for you; try to complete it by persuading the reader that a vegetarian lifestyle is a healthier option for families.

The first reason to adopt a vegetarian lifestyle is the benefits that it will have to the health of you and your loved ones. Whereas meat is scientifically proven to increase the risk of heart disease...

....

....

....

....

[3]

6 Now choose one of your own points from the table in question **3** and develop it into a paragraph, persuading families to adopt a vegetarian lifestyle. Using the previous example as a model, remember to start with a clear topic sentence and include a connective phrase to show development (such as Furthermore, In addition, Another reason, etc).

....

....

....

....

....

....

....

[4]

Total Marks .... / 27

Progress Test 2

1 What is a narrator?

[1]

....

2 Insert the correct phrase in each of the following sentences. Choose from:

first person	third person	intrusive	unreliable	naive

a) A .... narrative is any story told by someone in the story, using 'I'.   [1]

b) An .... narrator is one the reader may not be able to trust.   [1]

c) A .... narrative is one told by someone outside the story.   [1]

d) A .... narrator is one who does not always understand what is going on.   [1]

e) An .... narrator gives a commentary or opinion on what is happening.   [1]

Look at this writing task.

> 'Children's play areas are a safety risk and should be closed down.' Write an article for a national newspaper, presenting an argument about this topic.

3 **a)** What is the purpose, audience and form for this piece of writing?

....

....

[3]

b) What will you need to use to separate your different points?

....

[1]

c) What type of connectives will you need in this piece of writing?

....

....

[3]

4 Write a plan for this writing task. Some ideas have been included to get you started.

> No   Play areas are vital for children to socialise and have fun.
> Yes   Children are regularly injured playing on items such as climbing frames and slides.

[2]

5 Read the student response below.

There have resently been claims from different pressure groups that childrens play areas should be closed down. It has been suggested that they pose a risk to children's safety, although their are valid viewpoints on both sides, closing down such parks seems an extreme measure. Play areas provide to vital functions in the lives of young people they are a place to have fun and a place to socialise. While children must be kept safe, they must not spend their lives indoors and alone. Children develope by interacting with other children through acts of play, whether collaborative or competetive. Closing down areas that allow these activitys would damage the lives of children across the nation.

Using your plan, add another paragraph to continue the student's response.

....

....

....

....

....

....

[5]

6 Reread the student response given in question **5**. The content is good but the accuracy and organisation could be improved. Annotate the text with your corrections. Think about:

- paragraphing
- punctuation
- spelling
- grammar.

[10]

Read this extract from *Silas Marner* by George Eliot, written in 1861 but set fifty years earlier. Then answer the questions that follow.

In this extract the writer describes the village in which her story takes place.

It was an important-looking village, with a fine old church and large churchyard in the heart of it, and two or three large brick-and-stone homesteads, with well-walled orchards and ornamental weathercocks, standing close upon the road, and lifting more imposing fronts than the rectory,[1] which peeped from among the trees on the other side of the churchyard: – a village which showed at once the summits of its social life, and told the practised eye that there was no great park and manor-house in the vicinity, but that there were several chiefs in Raveloe who could farm badly quite at their ease, drawing enough money in those war times,[2] to live in a rollicking fashion, and keep a jolly Christmas, Whitsun and Easter tide.

[1] The name of a house where the rector or vicar lives

[2] Britain was at war with France from 1793 to 1815

7 List **four** things that can be seen in the village.

_____

_____ [4]

8 Explain what is meant by the following phrases and how they give the reader an impression of life in the village.

a) 'well-walled orchards and ornamental weathercocks'

_____

_____ [2]

b) 'more imposing fronts than the rectory'

_____

_____ [2]

c) 'a rollicking fashion'

_____

_____ [2]

9 This is a third person narrative. Explain the effect of using the third person here.

_____

_____ [2]

10 George Eliot has also been described as an intrusive narrator. How is this demonstrated in the given extract? Support your answer with details from the text.

....

....

....

....

....

[4]

11 Which of these statements do you think expresses the writer's attitude to the village? Tick **two**.

a) She describes the village with affection but does not think it is perfect. ☐

b) She loves the village and admires all the people who live there. ☐

c) She wants us to think the village is a terrible place to live. ☐

d) She uses irony to show that not everyone is hard-working or virtuous. ☐ [2]

12 How does the writer use language to show that religion is not as important as it might be to the people of Raveloe? Use details from the text in your answer.

....

....

....

....

....

[4]

13 How does the writer use language to convey the importance of the farmers of Raveloe?

....

....

....

....

....

[4]

Total Marks .... / 56

Writing 6

Writing to Persuade

1 Complete the FORESTRY mnemonic of persuasive techniques.

- F ....
- O ....
- R ....
- E ....
- S ....
- T ....
- R ....
- Y ....   [8]

2 Identify the different persuasive techniques from the FORESTRY mnemonic in this
paragraph. Annotate the text or write your answer on a separate piece of paper.

> Washing your hands is the simplest thing you can do to remain healthy as it gets rid
> of bacteria. It reduces the chance of stomach-related illnesses by 60%. All it takes is
> water, soap and twenty seconds. That's not difficult, is it? This ensures that you
> aren't putting your health, and the health of your friends and family, at
> perilous risk.

[8]

3 Which of the persuasive techniques used above do you think is the most effective at getting
people to wash their hands and why?

....

....

....   [1]

4 Write an extra sentence about handwashing, using the technique that you felt was most
effective.

....

....

....   [1]

5 Imagine you are creating an advertising campaign for a new product. This could be a pair of trainers, a chocolate bar, a deodorant, a console game, etc. Write **four** sentences about the product, each one using a different persuasive technique. Choose the **four** techniques that you think will be most effective in persuading people to buy your product.

- ....
- ....
- ....
- .... [4]

6 Think of something you dislike, such as a certain food, a subject at school or a type of television programme. Make a quick mindmap of the things you dislike about that topic.

[3]

7 To challenge your ability to write persuasively, write **three** sentences persuading people to **support** your chosen topic from question **6**. For example, if you decided that you dislike homework, you now need to write three sentences persuading your teachers to give you less homework! Each sentence should contain a different persuasive technique.

- ....
- ....
- .... [3]

Total Marks .... / 28

Writing 7

1 How is writing to argue similar and different from writing to persuade?

....

.... [2]

2 What features of writing to persuade could you make use of when writing to argue?

....

....

....

.... [4]

3 Practise forming a balanced argument by coming up with **three** points that **support** and **three** points that are **against** the following situations. An example has been given for you.

- The decision to close a local park because of criminal activity and anti-social behaviour.

For....	Against...
It will reduce crime.	However the crime may simply move to a different area.

- Young people being limited to one hour each night on their mobile phones.

For....	Against...

- Plans by your school to close at midday every Friday.

For....	Against...

[18]

4 When writing to argue, what type of connectives should you use and why?

[6]

5 Choose **one** of the scenarios in question **3** and write a clear topic sentence that introduces each of your points, for and against.

[6]

6 Develop **one** of your topic sentences (for) into a complete paragraph, making use of language techniques to successfully argue your point.

[4]

Total Marks .... / 40

Writing 8

1 When writing to advise, what are you trying to achieve?

.... [1]

2 Tick the box that best describes the tone you should use when writing to advise.

a) Clear and assertive ☐

b) Patient and kind ☐

c) Firm yet friendly ☐

d) Demanding and uncompromising ☐ [1]

3 Why is the second person ('you') so important in writing to advise?

....

.... [1]

4 Which **two** sentence types do you particularly need to use?

....

.... [2]

5 Why do you need to use connectives of sequence?

....

.... [1]

6 Give **four** varied examples of connectives of sequence.

....

....

....

.... [4]

7 What are modal verbs used to show?

....

.... [2]

8 Imagine you've been asked to advise someone about how to improve their marks in assessments. Write a simple sentence of advice for each of the modal verbs below.

Modal verb to use	Sentence advising how to improve assessment results
could	
must	
need	
ought	
should	

[5]

9 a) Complete a mindmap of different things you could advise someone to do if they want to lose weight and get fitter. [3]

b) Once you have finished, highlight your ideas in different colours to group them together (for example, you could group together all your ideas about changing diet). [1]

c) Look at your groupings, and the ideas within them, and consider how you could apply modal verbs. Which of your suggestions are vital (must/need), which are quite important (should/ought), and which are optional extras (could)? [1]

10 Write up one of your idea groups from question **9** into a full paragraph. Use the techniques of writing to advise in order to encourage the reader to follow your valuable advice. Write your answer on a separate piece of paper.

You might begin: *The first thing you need to do if you want to get fitter is...* [6]

Total Marks _____ / 28

Writing 9

Vocabulary and Sentences

1 Find **five** synonyms (alternative words) for each of these verbs.

look	say	eat	want

[20]

2 Find **five** synonyms for each of these adjectives.

good	bad	big	small

[20]

3 Choose **one** of the adjectives from question **2** and arrange your synonyms on a line of intensity to show you understand their different shades of meaning. For example, if one of the adjectives had been scary, you might have come up with:

creepy > unsettling > sinister > frightening > terrifying

_____ [1]

4 Rewrite this sentence twice, using different synonyms for the words in **bold**. To challenge yourself, you could make your first version very intense and your second version less intense.

> I **went** to the **big** party my friend was having; it was **loud** and **busy** but I **liked** the music and the company.

_____

_____

_____

_____ [10]

5 Give **two** reasons why you might use each of the following sentence structures.

    a) short, simple sentences

    b) compound sentences

    c) complex sentences

    d) lists

    [8]

6 Write a description of something exciting, such as riding a rollercoaster or opening birthday presents.

    Restrict yourself to **five** sentences: one simple, one compound, two complex and one list.

    Try to choose your sentence structures to achieve some of the effects that you identified in question **5**.

    [5]

Total Marks / 64

Writing 10

Writing to Inform

1. What sort of factual information might you include in writing to inform?

   ....

   ....

   .... [3]

2. Define the terms 'chronological' and 'thematic'.

   ....

   .... [2]

3. What **two** types of connectives are particularly important in writing to inform?

   .... [2]

4. Look carefully at the following information and number it so it is in chronological order.
   Put a number in each box.

   All the celebrities went to an after-show party. ☐

   Champagne and canapes were served before the film. ☐

   Everyone watched the film. ☐

   Famous people arrived in limousines. ☐

   There was applause because everyone enjoyed the film. ☐

   They had their photographs taken outside the doors to the cinema. ☐

   They walked along the red carpet to the film premiere. ☐ [7]

5. Now rewrite the sentences from question **4** into a paragraph, using a connective word or
   phrase at the start of each sentence.

   ....

   ....

   ....

   ....

   ....

   ....

   .... [7]

6 Read these two tasks and decide whether they would be best approached **chronologically** or **thematically**.

a) You write for your school newspaper and there has been a fire in the science block. Write an article for the newspaper, informing students about what happened.

_____ [1]

b) 'Arts' magazine is inviting young people to contribute an article about their favourite style of music. Write your article, informing readers about your opinion.

_____ [1]

7 Look at the question below then mindmap your ideas and group them thematically. Try to come up with **four** different groups of ideas.

Each week, your school website includes a feature about students' preferred charities. Write an article informing other students about the work of your chosen charity, how you have got involved and different ways they can support the charity.

[4]

8 Choose **one** of your sets of information from question **7** and write it up into a paragraph. Remember to include plenty of factual information and to incorporate connectives of time or place.

_____

_____

_____

_____

_____ [4]

Total Marks _____ / 31

Writing 11

Writing to Explain

1 How is writing to explain different from writing to inform?

.... [1]

2 Which of these tasks requires writing to inform and which requires writing to explain? Give a reason for your decision.

a) Your school magazine is running an anti-smoking campaign. Write an article about how smoking affects the health of your body.

.... [1]

b) A famous celebrity has recently completed the London Marathon to raise money for the charity that you work for. Write a report about the day to be posted on the charity's website.

.... [1]

3 Decide whether the following explanations are causes or effects.

	Topic	Explanation	Cause or effect?
a)	A long period without rainfall	Crops dry up and die	
b)	Revising effectively for exams	Good exam results	
c)	Suffering from anorexia	The pressure of slim body images in the media	
d)	Smoking	Lung disease	
e)	High blood pressure	Lack of exercise and an unhealthy diet	
f)	Tornados causing havoc across the country	Warm humid air colliding with cold dry air	

[6]

4 List **five** connectives that can show cause or effect.

....

.... [5]

5 In writing to explain, when should you use the present tense and when should you use the past tense?

....

.... [2]

6 Why are paragraphs and topic sentences important in writing to explain?

_____

_____ [2]

7 Plan a response to the question below; some ideas have been included to help you. Try to come up with **three** more main ideas, their causes or effects, and some examples or facts as supporting evidence.

> You work for a local newspaper. You have been asked to write an article for the weekend magazine about the benefits of getting young children to read for half an hour every day.

Point 1: Books improve children's knowledge and empathy.
Understanding of the world around you and others' perspectives, for example stories about people of different class, age, gender, background, etc.
Understanding of the past, such as life during WW2.

Reading

[6]

8 Choose **one** of your points from question **7** and turn it into a paragraph. Remember to support your ideas with evidence and to use connectives of cause or effect.

_____

_____

_____

_____ [4]

Total Marks _____ / 28

Writing 12

1 What is a simile and what is a metaphor?

_____

_____ [2]

2 Turn this metaphor into a simile: The fear turned my legs to stone.

_____ [1]

3 Turn this simile into a metaphor: Her words were like arrows fired at my heart.

_____ [1]

4 What is personification?

_____ [1]

5 Write a few sentences describing a derelict building. Include one simile, one metaphor and one example of personification.

_____

_____

_____

_____ [3]

6 What are the **five** senses?

_____

_____ [5]

7 Write a few sentences describing someone taking an apple from a tree and eating it. Use all of the five senses at least once.

_____

_____

_____

_____

_____ [5]

8 What **three** different sound techniques can you use in your writing?

_____

_____ [3]

9 Write a few sentences describing a thunderstorm. Include each of your **three** sound techniques that you gave for question **8**.

_____

_____

_____ [3]

10 Imagine you have been asked to describe a strange island. Plan your writing. Think about what different things you could describe and then group these into four main ideas.

[4]

11 Write up **one** of your groups of ideas from question **10** into a paragraph. Try to use interesting verbs, adjectives, and adverbs, as well as at least three descriptive techniques (such as metaphor or the senses).

_____

_____

_____

_____

_____

_____ [5]

Total Marks _____ / 33

Look at this writing task and answer the questions that follow.

> You have been invited to enter a writing competition, with the winner published in a national newspaper. Write a description inspired by this image.

1 **a)** What is the purpose, audience and form for this piece of writing?

_____

_____ [3]

b) What techniques of imagery can you include?

_____

_____ [3]

c) What senses can you try to include?

_____

_____ [5]

2 Write a plan for the response to the writing task. Some ideas have been included to get you started.

> *Opening ideas – sun and heat...*
> *Seeing a mirage...*

[2]

Read the student response below.

> Drifting awake I opened my eyes. A blinding light hit me like burning arrows and I quickly snaped my eyelids shut again. Gradually, I peaked through my lashes to see the bright sun overhead: a ball of fire hanging in a clear blue sky. It's rays was fierce against my face and allready I could feel my skin becoming uncomfortable the heat seemed to prickle my flesh like red-hot needles. Raising my trembling hands to sheild my eyes from the sun I began to look around to work out where I am.

3 The content of the student response is good but the accuracy could be improved. Annotate the text with your corrections. Think about:

- punctuation
- spelling
- grammar. [10]

4 Using your plan from question **2**, add another paragraph to continue the student's response. Write your answer on a separate piece of paper. [5]

5 Complete this writing task. Write your answer on a separate piece of paper.

Allow yourself 45 minutes. Spend the first five minutes planning your work and the last five minutes checking your accuracy of spelling, punctuation, and grammar.

> You have been invited to enter a school writing competition. Write a description based on the competition's theme of 'winter'. [30]

Read the two passages below and answer the questions that follow.

Source A

One of the top destinations of our diverse and exciting city is Oak Lane. Easily accessible by train or bus, this vibrant suburban street is full of delights for locals and tourists alike. In the day time you can enjoy a plethora of small shops, among them a bookshop, two galleries, a couple of places selling upmarket trinkets and several antique and/or vintage outlets. And there's no shortage of places to enjoy a relaxing chat over a cup of coffee or glass of wine. At night, the lane is positively buzzing. You'll be spoilt for choice. Whether you prefer an ornate Edwardian pub or a contemporary 'shabby chic' wine bar and whatever your preferred cuisine (Indian, Chinese, Thai, Turkish and Italian spring to mind) I can guarantee you'll find something that suits your taste and pocket and brings you back to the lane again and again.

Source B

When we were young we were often sent on messages by our mum to Oak Lane. There were shops on the main road but she preferred Oak Lane. It was that little bit closer and safer for us children, with no busy road to cross, and she liked the fact that most of the shops were long-established. The shopkeepers knew us and we knew them. Also, Oak Lane had always been a bit 'classier' or, as we'd say now, more 'upmarket'. You could get more or less anything you needed there. There were three greengrocers, two butchers, a fishmonger, a post office, a newsagent, a baker, a chemist, a chandler, a barber and two pubs (not that I ever went in them – there was a strict 'no children' rule back then). Most of them have gone now, as in most places, but I do miss them. Still, I'm as much to blame as the next shopper – I wouldn't be without my regular deliveries from the supermarket.

6 **Three** of the following statements are about Source A and **three** are about Source B. For each statement write the correct source in the box.

Source

a) The writer is keen to attract people to Oak Lane.

b) The writer is nostalgic about the lane.

c) The writer mentions a variety of restaurants and bars.

d) The writer used to shop in Oak Lane as a child.

e) The writer takes some blame for the changes in Oak Lane.

f) The writer thinks Oak Lane will appeal to all sorts of people.

g) The writer mentions a variety of restaurants and bars. [7]

7 Refer only to **Source A** for this answer. Write your answer on a separate piece of paper.

How does the writer use language to give a positive impression of Oak Lane? [8]

8 Refer only to **Source B** for this answer. Write your answer on a separate piece of paper.

How does the writer use language to convey what Oak Lane was like in the past? [8]

9 Now refer to **both** sources. Write your answer on a separate piece of paper.

Summarise the differences between Oak Lane now and Oak Lane as described in Source B. [8]

Look at this writing task and answer the questions that follow.

'Fast food should be banned from being sold.' Write a speech to be given on a local radio's mid-morning show, persuading listeners that fast food should be banned.

10 a) What is the purpose, audience and form for this piece of writing?

....

.... [3]

b) What should you do if you disagree with the statement in the question?

.... [1]

c) What persuasive techniques could you use in your response?

....

....

....

....

.... [8]

11 Write a plan for your response to the writing task. Some ideas have been included to get you started.

> *Unhealthy: high in salt, sugar, and saturated fat.*
> *Creates a lot of litter.*

[2]

12 Read the student response below.

The main reason fast food should be banned is that it is unhealthy. It is full of things that are bad for the body. This can affect weight and increase the risk of different diseases. Even items that seem healthy can be worse than expected. For example, salads are often accompanied by dressings that are high in calories while some fruit juices contain a lot of sugar. It is imperative that fast food is banned in order to create a healthier nation.

The student's response is accurately written but it isn't very persuasive. Annotate the text to include at least **three** persuasive techniques. You could think about using:

- second person
- rhetorical questions
- triplets.

[3]

13 Using your plan from question **11**, add another paragraph to continue the student's response. Write your answer on a separate piece of paper.

[5]

14 Complete this writing task. Write your answer on a separate piece of paper.

Allow yourself 45 minutes. Spend the first five minutes planning your work and the last five minutes checking your accuracy of spelling, punctuation and grammar.

> 'Schools should teach students about relaxation and stress relief.' Write a letter to the Education Minister, persuading them of this viewpoint.

[30]

Total Marks .... / 141

Shakespeare

A Midsummer Night's Dream: Relationships

1 Summarise the relationship at the start of the play between:

a) Hermia and Lysander

_____

_____ [1]

b) Hermia and Demetrius

_____

_____ [1]

c) Helena and Demetrius

_____

_____ [1]

2 What is Egeus's complaint to Theseus?

_____

_____ [1]

3 What is Theseus's decision?

_____

_____ [1]

4 What do Hermia and Lysander decide to do?

_____

_____ [1]

5 Why do Helena and Demetrius become involved?

_____

_____

_____ [2]

6 Summarise the relationship at the start of the play between:

a) Peter Quince and Nick Bottom

....

.... [1]

b) Oberon and Titania

....

.... [1]

7 Why do the Mechanicals go to the forest?

....

.... [1]

8 What trick do Oberon and Puck play on Titania?

....

.... [1]

9 What does Oberon tell Puck to do to Demetrius and how does he get it wrong?

....

....

.... [2]

10 What are the consequences of Puck's mistake and how is it remedied?

....

....

.... [2]

11 In what ways does the play have a happy ending?

....

....

....

.... [3]

Total Marks .... / 19

Shakespeare

A Midsummer Night's Dream: The Lovers and Romance

1 Analyse how this extract from Demetrius's speech from Act 1 Scene 1 shows his attitude towards Hermia.

> DEMETRIUS   Relent, sweet Hermia; and, Lysander, yield
>   Thy crazed title to my certain right.

[2]

2 Analyse how this extract from Hermia and Helena's speeches from Act 1 Scene 1 presents a romantic problem.

> HERMIA   I give him curses; yet he gives me love.
> HELENA   O that my prayers could such affection move!

[2]

3 Analyse how Helena's speech from Act 2 Scene 1 presents her feelings of unrequited love.

> HELENA   Use me but as your spaniel, spurn me, strike me,
>   Neglect me, lose me; only give me leave,
>   Unworthy as I am, to follow you.

[3]

4 Analyse how Lysander's speech from Act 2 Scene 2 shows his love for Hermia.

> LYSANDER   I mean that my heart unto yours is knit
>   So that but one heart we can make of it;
>   Two bosoms interchanged with an oath;

[3]

5 Analyse how this extract from Act 3 Scene 2 presents the changes in Demetrius and Helena's relationship due to Puck's love spell.

DEMETRIUS	*[Waking]* O Helen, goddess, nymph, perfect, divine!
	To what, my love, shall I compare thine eyne?
	Crystal is muddy. O, how ripe in show
	Thy lips, those kissing cherries, tempting grow! [...]
HELENA	O spite! O hell! I see you are all bent
	To set against me for your merriment.

[4]

6 Compare how these extracts from Act 1 Scene 1 and Act 3 Scene 2 present the relationship between Lysander and Hermia. Write your answer on a separate piece of paper.

LYSANDER	There gentle Hermia, may I marry thee [...]
	And in the wood, a league without the town
	(Where I did meet thee once with Helena
	To do observance to a morn of May),
	There will I stay for thee.
HERMIA	My good Lysander!
	I swear to thee by Cupid's strongest bow,
	By his best arrow with the golden head,
	By the simplicity of Venus' doves,
	....
LYSANDER	Hang off, thou cat, thou burr! Vile thing, let loose,
	Or I will shake thee from me like a serpent!
HERMIA	Why are you grown so rude? what change is this,
	Sweet love?
LYSANDER	Thy love? Out, tawny Tartar, out!
	Out loathed medicine! O hated poison, hence!

[6]

Total Marks .... / 20

Shakespeare

A Midsummer Night's Dream: The Fairies and Magic

1 Analyse how Puck's speech from Act 2 Scene 2 presents his relationship with Oberon.

> PUCK   I jest to Oberon and make him smile [...]
> Fear not, my lord, your servant shall do so.

....

....

....

[2]

2 Analyse how Shakespeare presents Titania and Oberon's relationship in this extract from Act 2 Scene 1.

> OBERON   Ill met by moonlight, proud Titania.
> TITANIA   What, jealous Oberon? Fairies, skip hence;
> I have forsworn his bed and company.
> OBERON   Tarry, rash wanton; am I not thy Lord?

....

....

....

[3]

3 Analyse how Shakespeare presents Oberon's trick on Titania in this extract from Act 3 Scene 1.

> TITANIA   What angel wakes me from my flowery bed? [...]
> Thou art as wise as thou art beautiful.

....

....

....

[2]

4 Analyse how Puck and Oberon's speech from Act 3 Scene 2 shows their enjoyment of the trick on Titania.

> PUCK   When in that moment, so it came to pass,
> Titania wak'd, and straightway lov'd an ass.
> OBERON   This falls out better than I could devise.

....

....

....

[2]

5 Analyse how Puck engages with the audience at the end of the play in this extract from Act 5.

PUCK   you have but slumbered here
                While these visions did appear

_____

_____

_____

_____

[2]

6 Analyse how this extract from Act 2 Scene 1 presents the effects of Oberon and Titania's conflict. Write your answer on a separate piece of paper.

TITANIA   Therefore the winds, piping to us in vain,
                As in revenge have suck'd up from the sea
                Contagious fogs; which, falling in the land,
                Hath every pelting river made so proud
                That they have overborne their continents. [...]
                The seasons alter: hoary-headed frosts
                Fall in the fresh lap of the crimson rose,

[4]

7 Compare how these extracts from Act 2 Scene 1 and Act 4 Scene 1 present the relationship between Oberon and Titania. Write your answer on a separate piece of paper.

OBERON   Give me that boy, and I will go with thee.
TITANIA   Not for thy fairy kingdom. Fairies, away!
                We shall chide downright if I stay longer.
                [Exeunt Titania and her Train]
OBERON   Well, go thy way; thou shalt not from this grove
                Till I torment thee for this injury.

                ....

OBERON   Then my queen, in silence sad,
                Trip we after night's shade:
                We the globe can compass soon,
                Swifter than the wandering moon.
TITANIA   Come my lord, and in our flight
                Tell me how it came this night
                That I sleeping here was found
                With these mortals on the ground

[6]

Total Marks .... / 21

Shakespeare

A Midsummer Night's Dream: **The Mechanicals and Comedy**

1 Analyse how Quince's speech from Act 1 Scene 2 presents the Mechanicals as comic characters.

> QUINCE   to play in our interlude before the Duke and Duchess,
> on his wedding day at night. [...]
> Marry our play is 'The most lamentable comedy,
> and most cruel death of Pyramus and Thisbe.'

[2]

2 Analyse how Flute's speech from Act 1 Scene 2 is used to create comedy.

> FLUTE   Nay, faith, let me not play a woman: I have a beard coming.

[2]

3 Analyse how Quince and Bottom's speech from Act 1 Scene 2 is used to create comedy.

> BOTTOM   And I may hide my face, let me play Thisbe too.
> I'll speak in a monstrous little voice: 'Thisne
> Thisne!' – 'Ah, Pyramus, my lover dear! thy Thisbe
> dear, and lady dear!'
>
> QUINCE   No, no, you must play Pyramus; and Flute, you Thisbe.
>
> BOTTOM   Well, proceed.

[3]

4 Analyse how Shakespeare uses the transformation of Bottom to create comedy on stage in this extract from Act 3 Scene 1.

> QUINCE   Pyramus, enter! Your cue is past; it is 'never tire'.
>
> FLUTE   O – 'As true as truest horse that yet would never tire'.
> *[Enter Bottom with the ass-head on]*
>
> BOTTOM   If I were fair, Thisbe, I were only thine.
>
> QUINCE   O monstrous! O strange! We are haunted! Pray,
> masters! Fly, masters! Help!

[3]

5 Analyse how this extract from the Mechanicals' play from Act 5 Scene 1 is used to create comedy. Write your answer on a separate piece of paper.

QUINCE	If we offend, it is with our good will.
	That you should think, we come not to offend,
	But with good will. To show our simple skill,
	That is the true beginning of our end. […]
THESEUS	This fellow doth not stand upon points.
LYSANDER	He hath rid his prologue like a rough colt; he knows not the stop.

[4]

6 Compare how these extracts from Act 3 Scene 1 and Act 5 Scene 1 present Bottom. Write your answer on a separate piece of paper.

BOTTOM	'Thisbe, the flowers of odious savours sweet' –
QUINCE	'Odorous'! 'Odorous'!
BOTTOM	'Odorous savours sweet;
	So hath my breath, my dearest Thisbe dear.
	But hark, a voice! Stay thou but here awhile,
	And by and by, I will appear to thee'.
	[Exit]
PUCK	A stranger Pyramus than e'er played here!
	....
BOTTOM	*Thy mantle good,*
[as Pyramus]	*What! Stain'd with blood?*
	Approach, ye Furies fell!
	O Fates, come, come!
	Cut thread and thrum:
	Quail, crush, conclude, and quell.
THESEUS	This passion, and the death of a dear friend, would go near to make a man look sad.
HIPPOLYTA	Beshrew my heart, but I pity the man.

[6]

Total Marks _____ / 20

Shakespeare

The Tempest: Relationships

1 Summarise the relationship at the start of the play between:

a) Prospero and Ariel

....

.... [1]

b) Prospero and Caliban

....

.... [1]

c) Prospero and Miranda

....

.... [1]

d) Prospero, Antonio and Alonso

....

.... [1]

e) Prospero and Gonzalo

....

.... [1]

2 Why does Prospero organise the shipwreck?

....

.... [1]

3 How do Sebastian and Antonio plot against Alonso and Gonzalo?

....

.... [1]

4 Summarise the relationship between Stephano, Trinculo and Caliban.

....

.... [1]

5 Why does Prospero treat Ferdinand so harshly?

....

.... [1]

6 How does Prospero punish Stephano, Caliban and Trinculo?

....

.... [1]

7 What does Prospero feel for Antonio, Alonso and Sebastian at the end of the play?

....

.... [1]

8 How does Prospero reward Ariel at the end of the play?

....

.... [1]

9 How do Prospero and Alonso make amends with each other?

....

.... [1]

Total Marks .... / 13

Shakespeare

1 Analyse how Prospero's speech from Act 1 Scene 2 shows his control over Ariel.

> PROSPERO   Hast thou, spirit,
> Performed to point the tempest that I bade thee?

[2]

2 Analyse how Prospero's speech from Act 1 Scene 2 shows his control over Caliban.

> PROSPERO   Hag-seed, hence:
> Fetch us in fuel, and be quick

[2]

3 Analyse how Caliban's speech from Act 1 Scene 2 shows his feelings for Prospero.

> CALIBAN   [*aside*] I must obey; his art is of such power
> It would control my dam's god Setebos

[3]

4 Analyse how Ariel's speech from Act 1 Scene 2 shows his feelings for Prospero.

> ARIEL   All hail, great master; grave sir, hail! I come
> To answer thy best pleasure

[3]

5 Analyse how this extract from Act 4 Scene 1 presents the relationship between Prospero and Caliban.

PROSPERO	A devil, a born devil, on whose nature
	Nurture can never stick; on whom my pains
	Humanely taken – all, all lost, quite lost!
	And, as with age his body uglier grows,
	So his mind cankers. I will plague them all,
	Even to roaring. Come, hang them on this line.

[Enter Ariel, loaden with glistering apparel, etc. Enter Caliban, Stephano, and Trinculo, all wet.]

| CALIBAN | Pray you tread softly, that the blind mole may |
| | Not hear a footfall. We now are near his cell. |

[4]

6 Compare how these extracts from Act 1 Scene 2 and Act 4 Scene 1 present the relationship between Prospero and Ariel. Write your answer on a separate piece of paper.

PROSPERO	If thou more murmur'st, I will rend an oak
	And peg thee in his knotty entrails till
	Thou has howled away twelve winters.
ARIEL	Pardon, master,
	I will be correspondent to command
	....
ARIEL	*[singing]* Merrily, merrily, shall I live now,
	Under the blossom that hangs on the bough.
PROSPERO	Why, that's my dainty Ariel! I shall miss thee,
	But yet thou shalt have freedom. – So, so, so. –
	To the King's ship, invisible as thou art;

[6]

Total Marks _____ / 20

Shakespeare

The Tempest: Miranda and Ferdinand

1 Analyse how Miranda's speech from Act 1 Scene 2 shows her initial thoughts about Ferdinand.

> MIRANDA   I might call him
> A thing divine, for nothing natural
> I ever saw so noble.

[2]

2 Analyse how Prospero's words from Act 1 Scene 2 show his thoughts about Miranda and Ferdinand's relationship.

> PROSPERO   [*aside*] They are both in either's powers, but this swift business
> I must uneasy make, lest too light winning
> Make the prize light.

[3]

3 Analyse how this extract from Act 3 Scene 1 presents the relationship between Miranda and Ferdinand.

> FERDINAND   O most dear mistress,
> The sun will set before I shall discharge
> What I must strive to do.
>
> MIRANDA   If you'll sit down,
> I'll bear your logs the while. Pray give me that;
> I'll carry it to the pile.
>
> FERDINAND   No, precious creature,
> I had rather crack my sinews, break my back,
> Than you should such dishonour undergo
> While I sit lazy by.

[4]

Total Marks _____ / 9

The Tempest: Alonso and Gonzalo

1 Analyse how Gonzalo's speech from Act 2 Scene 1 to Alonso after the shipwreck shows he is optimistic.

GONZALO   Beseech you, sir, be merry. You have cause
(So have we all) of joy, for our escape
Is much beyond our loss.

[2]

2 Analyse how Alonso's words from Act 1 Scene 2 show his thoughts about losing Ferdinand.

ALONSO   Even here I will put off my hope and keep it
No longer for my flatterer. He is drowned
Whom thus we stray to find, and the sea mocks
Our frustrate search on land. Well, let him go.

[3]

3 Analyse how this extract from Act 5 Scene 1 presents the relationship between Prospero and Alonso.

PROSPERO   Behold, sir King,
The wronged Duke of Milan, Prospero!
For more assurance that a living prince
Does now speak to thee, I embrace thy body,
And to thee and thy company I bid
A hearty welcome. [...]

ALONSO   Thy dukedom I resign and do entreat
Thou pardon me my wrongs. But how should Prospero
Be living, and be here?

[4]

Total Marks .... / 9

Shakespeare

1 Analyse how Ariel's speech (to Prospero) from Act 1 Scene 2 presents him as a magical character.

ARIEL	To fly
	To swim, to dive into the fire, to ride
	On the curled clouds.

[2]

2 Analyse how Prospero's speech (to Caliban) from Act 1 Scene 2 presents his magical powers.

PROSPERO	For this, be sure, tonight thou shalt have cramps,
	Side-stitches, that shall pen thy breath up.

[2]

3 Analyse how Sebastian's speech (to Antonio) from Act 2 Scene 1 shows corruption.

SEBASTIAN	Thy case, dear friend,
	Shall be my precedent. As thou got'st Milan,
	I'll come by Naples. Draw thy sword!

[3]

4 Analyse how Sebastian and Antonio's speech from Act 3 Scene 3 shows corruption.

SEBASTIAN	The next advantage
[aside to Antonio]	Will we take thoroughly.
ANTONIO	Let it be tonight,
[aside to Sebastian]	For now they are oppressed with travail; they
	Will not, not cannot use such vigilance
	As when they are fresh.

[3]

5 Analyse how this extract of Prospero's speech from Act 5, Scene 1 presents magical powers.

> PROSPERO   to the dread rattling thunder
> Have I given fire and rifted Jove's stout oak
> With his own bolt; the strong-based promontory
> Have I made shake and by the spurs pluck'd up
> The pine and cedar: graves at my command
> Have waked their sleepers, oped, and let 'em forth
> By my so potent art. But this rough magic
> I here abjure.

[4]

6 Compare how these extracts from Act 3 Scene 3 and Act 5 Scene 1 present corruption. Write your answer on a separate piece of paper.

> ARIEL   You are three men of sin, whom Destiny,
> That hath to instrument this lower world
> And what is in't, the never-surfeited sea
> Hath caused to belch up you; and on this island
> Where man doth not inhabit; you 'mongst men
> Being most unfit to live.
>
> ....
>
> PROSPERO   You, brother mine, that entertain'd ambition,
> Expell'd remorse and nature; who, with Sebastian,
> Whose inward pinches therefore are most strong,
> Would here have kill'd your king; I do forgive thee,
> Unnatural though thou art.

[6]

Total Marks   / 20

Look at this writing task and answer the questions that follow.

> 'Social media is difficult for the older generation to understand.' Write a guide informing people who are over 60 about social media.

1 a) What is the purpose, audience and form for this piece of writing?

....

....

.... [3]

b) Does this type of writing require more **facts** or more **opinions**? .... [1]

c) Should the writing task be approached chronologically or thematically?

.... [1]

2 Write a plan for this response. Some ideas have been included to get you started.

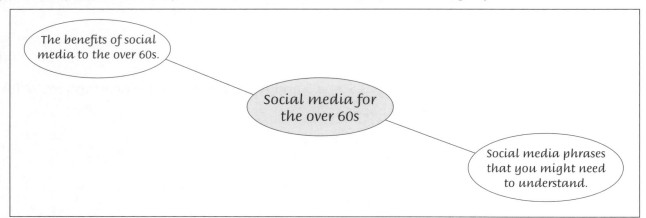

The benefits of social media to the over 60s.

Social media for the over 60s

Social media phrases that you might need to understand.

[2]

3 Read the student response below.

> My favourite social media word is obviously going to be 'like'. This is the way in which you show approval for something that has been posted. It's a great feeling when someone likes something you have done. The best things to like are other people's 'selfies'. If you have never heard this term, it's when you take a photograph of yourself doing something fun or interesting. Taking selfies is so much fun.
>
> One benefit of social media is that you can keep in touch with people all the time. This is wonderful to be able to do. I think the best way to keep in touch is through WhatsApp but there are lots of other really good options and I know people who still love Facebook.

The piece is written accurately but it is too opinionated and the ideas are not introduced clearly. Alter the text to make it more fact-based and include topic sentences. If needed, write your answer on a separate piece of paper. [3]

4 Using your plan from question **2**, add another paragraph to continue the student's response.

....

....

....

....

....

[5]

5 Starting with this extract (Act 2 Scene 2, lines 1–17) from *The Tempest*, analyse how Shakespeare presents Caliban's relationship with Prospero in the play. Write your answer on a separate piece of paper.

[Enter CALIBAN with a burden of wood. A noise of thunder heard]

CALIBAN	All the infections that the sun sucks up
	From bogs, fens, flats, on Prosper fall and make him
	By inch-meal a disease! His spirits hear me
	And yet I needs must curse. But they'll nor pinch,
	Fright me with urchin--shows, pitch me i' the mire,
	Nor lead me, like a firebrand, in the dark
	Out of my way, unless he bid 'em; but
	For every trifle are they set upon me;
	Sometime like apes that mow and chatter at me
	And after bite me, then like hedgehogs which
	Lie tumbling in my barefoot way and mount
	Their pricks at my footfall; sometime am I
	All wound with adders who with cloven tongues
	Do hiss me into madness.

[Enter TRINCULO]

	Lo, now, lo!
	Here comes a spirit of his, and to torment me
	For bringing wood in slowly. I'll fall flat;
	Perchance he will not mind me.

[20]

6 Starting with this extract (Act 1 Scene 1, lines 180–197) from *A Midsummer Night's Dream*, analyse how Shakespeare presents Helen and Hermia's relationship in the play. Write your answer on a separate piece of paper.

HERMIA	God speed fair Helena! whither away?
HELENA	Call you me fair? that fair again unsay.
	Demetrius loves your fair: O happy fair!
	Your eyes are lode-stars; and your tongue's sweet air
	More tuneable than lark to shepherd's ear,
	When wheat is green, when hawthorn buds appear.
	Sickness is catching: O, were favour so,
	Yours would I catch, fair Hermia, ere I go;
	My ear should catch your voice, my eye your eye,
	My tongue should catch your tongue's sweet melody.
	Were the world mine, Demetrius being bated,

The rest I'd give to be to you translated.
O, teach me how you look, and with what art
You sway the motion of Demetrius' heart.

HERMIA	I frown upon him, yet he loves me still.
HELENA	O that your frowns would teach my smiles such skill!
HERMIA	I give him curses, yet he gives me love.
HELENA	O that my prayers could such affection move!
HERMIA	The more I hate, the more he follows me.
HELENA	The more I love, the more he hateth me.

[20]

Read this review, which was published in the *Liverpool Echo* in 1914, and answer the questions that follow.

Tivoli Theatre, New Brighton

New Brighton's latest and most cosy little variety theatre was packed at both performances last night, and Mr. H. M. Moore, the manager, is to be complimented upon being able to present such a good array of turns, which are all excellent. The principal item is provided by Tatton Hall, in Clarke and Hamilton's Revue, a most mirth-provoking affair. Nelson Jackson is already popular, and his entertainment at the piano last evening was as amusing and smart ever. T. C. Eric is an exceptionally clever ventriloquist. Royde and Villiers were seen to marked effect in comedy and harmony. Yazo, assisted by Mdlle. Leclere, rendered most beautifully some selections on the violin. The remainder of the company included Harvard and Little Lady, Monty Ash, a smart comedian, and the Dancing Duggans, a set of vocalists and dancers.

---

7 Which 'turn' or act...

a) played the violin? _____ [1]

b) was a ventriloquist? _____ [1]

c) danced? _____ [1]

d) played the piano? _____ [1]

8 What could be inferred about the acts mentioned in the final sentence from its beginning 'the remainder of the company'? Pick **two** answers.

a) The writer did not enjoy them as much as the other turns.   ☐

b) The writer thought they were excellent and so mentions them last.   ☐

c) Their acts are not easily described.   ☐

d) They are less well known and are therefore further down the bill.   ☐   [2]

9 How is the article structured to interest the reader?

....

....

....

....   [4]

10 What is the purpose of the article?

....

....   [2]

11 In your own words, summarise the writer's view of the evening.

....

....

....

....   [4]

12 How does the writer use language to express this view?

....

....

....

....   [4]

13 Complete this writing task.

Allow yourself 45 minutes. Spend the first five minutes planning your work and the last five minutes checking your accuracy of spelling, punctuation and grammar. Write your answer on a separate piece of paper.

> Write the opening of a story, to be published on a national creative writing website, using the title 'The Haunted Toyshop'.

[30]

14 Starting with this extract (Act 3 Scene 1, lines 68–86) from *The Tempest*, analyse how Shakespeare presents the theme of romantic love in the play. Write your answer on a separate piece of paper.

MIRANDA	Do you love me?
FERDINAND	O heaven, O earth, bear witness to this sound And crown what I profess with kind event If I speak true! if hollowly, invert What best is boded me to mischief! I Beyond all limit of what else i' the world Do love, prize, honour you.
MIRANDA	I am a fool To weep at what I am glad of.
PROSPERO	[aside] Fair encounter Of two most rare affections! Heavens rain grace On that which breeds between 'em!
FERDINAND	Wherefore weep you?
MIRANDA	At mine unworthiness that dare not offer What I desire to give, and much less take What I shall die to want. But this is trifling; And all the more it seeks to hide itself, The bigger bulk it shows. Hence, bashful cunning! And prompt me, plain and holy innocence! I am your wife, if you will marry me; If not, I'll die your maid: to be your fellow You may deny me; but I'll be your servant, Whether you will or no.

[20]

15 Starting with this extract (Act 2 Scene 1, lines 169–187), from *A Midsummer Night's Dream*, analyse how Shakespeare presents magic in the play. Write your answer on a separate piece of paper.

OBERON	Fetch me that flower; the herb I shew'd thee once:
	The juice of it on sleeping eye-lids laid
	Will make or man or woman madly dote
	Upon the next live creature that it sees.
	Fetch me this herb; and be thou here again
	Ere the leviathan can swim a league.
PUCK	I'll put a girdle round about the earth
	In forty minutes.

[Exit]

OBERON	Having once this juice,
	I'll watch Titania when she is asleep,
	And drop the liquor of it in her eyes.
	The next thing then she waking looks upon,
	Be it on lion, bear, or wolf, or bull,
	On meddling monkey, or on busy ape,
	She shall pursue it with the soul of love:
	And ere I take this charm from off her sight,
	As I can take it with another herb,
	I'll make her render up her page to me.
	But who comes here? I am invisible;
	And I will overhear their conference.

[20]

16 Complete this writing task.

Allow yourself 45 minutes. Spend the first five minutes planning your work and the last five minutes checking your accuracy of spelling, punctuation and grammar. Write your answer on a separate piece of paper.

> 'More money should be spent by local councils on providing leisure activities for teenagers'. Write an article for your local newspaper, providing a balanced argument about this issue.

[30]

Total Marks _____ / 175

Mixed Test-Style Questions

Reading: Fiction

This text is the opening of *Kidnapped*, a novel for children by Robert Louis Stevenson, first published in 1886.

Spend about 15 minutes reading the text before answering all the questions that follow.

You should take about 45 minutes to complete it, dividing your time appropriately between the questions.

I will begin the story of my adventures with a certain morning early in the month of June, the year of grace 1751, when I took the key for the last time out of the door of my father's house. The sun began to shine upon the summit of the hills as I went down the road; and by the time I had come as far as the manse[1], the blackbirds were whistling in the garden lilacs, and the mist that hung around
5   the valley in the time of the dawn was beginning to arise and die away.

Mr. Campbell, the minister of Essendean, was waiting for me by the garden gate, good man! He asked me if I had breakfasted; and hearing that I lacked for nothing, he took my hand in both of his and clapped it kindly under his arm.

"Well, Davie, lad," said he, "I will go with you as far as the ford, to set you on the way." And we
10   began to walk forward in silence.

"Are ye sorry to leave Essendean?" said he, after a while.

"Why, sir," said I, "if I knew where I was going, or what was likely to become of me, I would tell you candidly. Essendean is a good place indeed, and I have been very happy there; but then I have never been anywhere else. My father and mother, since they are both dead, I shall be no nearer to
15   in Essendean than in the Kingdom of Hungary, and, to speak truth, if I thought I had a chance to better myself where I was going I would go with a good will."

"Ay?" said Mr. Campbell. "Very well, Davie. Then it behoves me[2] to tell your fortune; or so far as I may. When your mother was gone, and your father (the worthy, Christian man) began to sicken for his end, he gave me in charge a certain letter, which he said was your inheritance. 'So soon,' says
20   he, 'as I am gone, and the house is redd up and the gear disposed of' (all which, Davie, hath been done), 'give my boy this letter into his hand, and start him off to the house of Shaws, not far from Cramond. That is the place I came from,' he said, 'and it's where it befits that my boy should return. He is a steady lad,' your father said, 'and a canny[3] goer; and I doubt not he will come safe, and be well lived where he goes.'"

25   "The house of Shaws!" I cried. "What had my poor father to do with the house of Shaws?"

"Nay," said Mr. Campbell, "who can tell that for a surety? But the name of that family, Davie, boy, is the name you bear – Balfours of Shaws: an ancient, honest, reputable house, peradventure in these latter days decayed. Your father, too, was a man of learning as befitted his position; no man more plausibly conducted school; nor had he the manner or the speech of a common dominie[4]; but
30   (as ye will yourself remember) I took aye a pleasure to have him to the manse to meet the gentry; and those of my own house, Campbell of Kilrennet, Campbell of Dunswire, Campbell of Minch,

and others, all well-kenned[5] gentlemen, had pleasure in his society. Lastly, to put all the elements of this affair before you, here is the testamentary letter itself, superscrived[6] by the own hand of our departed brother."

35 He gave me the letter, which was addressed in these words: "To the hands of Ebenezer Balfour, Esquire, of Shaws, in his house of Shaws, these will be delivered by my son, David Balfour." My heart was beating hard at this great prospect now suddenly opening before a lad of seventeen years of age, the son of a poor country dominie in the Forest of Ettrick.

"Mr. Campbell," I stammered, "and if you were in my shoes, would you go?"

[1] manse – the home of the minister
[2] it behoves me – I should
[3] canny – clever
[4] dominie – teacher
[5] well-kenned – well-known
[6] superscrived – written on the top or the outside of a letter

1 Look again at the first paragraph.

List **four** aspects of nature that the narrator notices on his walk.

....

....

4 marks

Write your answers to questions **2**, **3** and **4** on separate pieces of paper.

2 Look in detail at this extract from the source (lines 1 to 8).

I will begin the story of my adventures with a certain morning early in the month of June, the year of grace 1751, when I took the key for the last time out of the door of my father's house. The sun began to shine upon the summit of the hills as I went down the road; and by the time I had come as far as the manse[1], the blackbirds were whistling in the garden lilacs, and the mist that hung around the valley in the time of the dawn was beginning to arise and die away.

Mr. Campbell, the minister of Essendean, was waiting for me by the garden gate, good man! He asked me if I had breakfasted; and hearing that I lacked for nothing, he took my hand in both of his and clapped it kindly under his arm.

How does the writer use language to create a mood of optimism and hope?

You could include the writer's choice of:

- words and phases
- language features and techniques
- sentence forms.

8 marks

Mixed Test-Style Questions

3 You now need to think about the whole of the source. This text is the opening of a novel.

How has the writer structured the text to interest you as a reader?

You could write about:

- what the writer focuses your attention on at the beginning of the text
- how and why he changes this focus as the story develops
- any other structural features that interest you.

8 marks

4 Focus your answer on the second part of the source from line 17 ("Ay?" said Mr. Campbell...) to the end.

A student has said, 'At the beginning of the story, Stevenson makes us wonder about Davie's father's background, and makes us wants to find out more about the letter he has left and the mysterious Shaw family.'

To what extent do you agree?

In your response you could:

- consider your own impressions of Davie's father and Mr Campbell's account of him
- evaluate how the writer tells us about his background and what he has told Mr Campbell
- support your response with references to the text.

20 marks

TOTAL

40

Reading: Poetry

Read this poem, written by Oliver Goldsmith in 1770, and answer the questions that follow.

Spend about 15 minutes reading the text before answering all the questions that follow.

You should take about 45 minutes to complete it, dividing your time appropriately between the questions.

The Village Schoolmaster

Beside yon straggling fence that skirts the way
With blossom'd furze unprofitably gay,
There, in his noisy mansion, skill'd to rule,
The village master taught his little school;
5 A man severe he was, and stern to view,
I knew him well, and every truant knew;
Well had the boding[1] tremblers learn'd to trace
The days disasters in his morning face;
Full well they laugh'd with counterfeited glee,
10 At all his jokes, for many a joke had he:
Full well the busy whisper, circling round,
Convey'd the dismal tidings when he frown'd:
Yet he was kind; or if severe in aught,
The love he bore to learning was in fault.
15 The village all declar'd how much he knew;
'Twas certain he could write, and cipher[2] too:
Lands he could measure, terms and tides presage[3],
And e'en the story ran that he could gauge.
In arguing too, the parson own'd his skill,
20 For e'en though vanquish'd he could argue still;
While words of learned length and thund'ring sound
Amazed the gazing rustics rang'd around;
And still they gaz'd and still the wonder grew,
That one small head could carry all he knew.
25 But past is all his fame. The very spot
Where many a time he triumph'd is forgot.

[1] boding – worrying about what might happen
[2] cipher – to do arithmetic
[3] presage – foretell

Mixed Test-Style Questions

1 Look again at lines 1 to 6.

List **four** words or phrases that tell us about the subject of the poem.

....

....

4 marks

Write your answers to questions **2**, **3** and **4** on separate pieces of paper.

2 Look in detail at the source from lines 5 to 14 ('A man severe he was...' to '...learning he was in fault.').

How does the writer use language to convey the character of the schoolmaster and the atmosphere in his school?

You could include the writer's choice of:

- words and phases
- language features and techniques
- sentence forms.

8 marks

3 You now need to think about the whole of the source.

How has the writer structured the poem to interest you as a reader?

You could write about:

- what the writer focuses your attention on at the beginning of the poem
- how and why he changes this focus as the poem develops
- any other structural features that interest you.

8 marks

4 Focus your answer on the second part of the source from line 13 to the end.

A student has said, 'In this poem Goldsmith conveys a vivid picture of a man who is respected and loved by his community.'

To what extent do you agree?

In your response you could:

- consider your own impressions of the village schoolmaster
- evaluate how the writer tells us about his character and how the villagers react to him
- support your response with references to the text.

20 marks

TOTAL

40

Reading: Non-Fiction

On these pages you there are two non-fiction texts on similar subjects. One was written in the nineteenth century and the other in the twenty-first century.

Spend about 15 minutes reading the two texts before answering all the questions that follow.

You should take about 45 minutes to complete it, dividing your time appropriately between the questions.

Source A

In this article, the writer describes his unfortunate reaction to cats.

It's All Your Fault, Stan! by Dan Featherstone

Now, let's get one thing straight from the start. I don't hate cats. I'll repeat that just in case any cat lovers out there (and I know there are millions of you) are thinking of sending me abusive messages. I don't hate cats. I don't even dislike them. They don't like me.

5   Well, to be fair to the cats, they don't really know they don't like me – or at least I hope they don't. If they are aware of their effect on me, they really are vindictive, and I don't want to think that because I actually used to quite like them. As children we always had cats. They suited us. They made themselves useful round the house, dealing with mice and other unwanted visitors. Unlike dogs, they were very easy to care for, though I'm not sure if 'care for' is the right phrase.

10   They mostly took care of themselves. And they could be quite affectionate or even entertaining. One of them, a huge ginger creature called Stan (after the butcher) seemed particularly anxious not to lose us. In the morning he would try to come to school with us, following us up the road as far as the bus stop. I'm sure that if he'd had the money for his fare, he would have got on with us. When we got back, he'd meet us half way down the street. He didn't walk with us – that would

15   have been uncool – but went through all the neighbours' front gardens, leaping over small stone walls and ornamental shrubs with an agility that belied this appearance.

Unfortunately, it is Stan that I hold responsible for my troubles. Before I met him, I was not allergic to cats. I was not allergic to anything. When he first arrived, I was fine. By the time I left (yes, of course I left home – you couldn't expect Stan to) I had all the symptoms: running nose,

20   coughing, wheezing, itching, unsightly rashes. You name it, I had it. The only thing that helped my symptoms was staying away from Stan.

At first, I thought it was only Stan but then other cats got in on the act. For some reason, whenever I visited a friend or relative who had a cat, it would make a beeline for me, rubbing against my legs or, even worse, jumping onto my lap. I would dread going to some people's

25   houses. How can you ask them to banish their best friend from its own home? But in the end that was what I had to do and now friends know that if they want my company, the cat will have to go elsewhere for its amusement. I haven't lost that many friends.

I still quite like cats – from a distance – and I do occasionally miss their company. Still, I can always watch documentaries about big cats in the wild and I do spend far too much time on the
30 computer watching those videos of cats making fools of themselves. I laugh far too loudly at them. It's my way of getting back at Stan.

Source B

This is a newspaper article that appeared in the *Huddersfield Chronicle* on 8 December 1879. In it the writer, 'JH,' remembers her childhood pet.

A TALE OF MY CAT

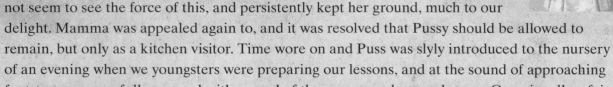

One day a poor, miserable-looking creature came mewing to our door; she was in the intermediate state of cat and kitten. Our maid-of-all-work took pity on her and gave her some milk, and as soon as we juveniles came home from school we were introduced to our new friend. Our mother, though the kindest of mortals,
5 had a horror of cats, so we were at once told that Pussy must be off. Pussy did not seem to see the force of this, and persistently kept her ground, much to our delight. Mamma was appealed again to, and it was resolved that Pussy should be allowed to remain, but only as a kitchen visitor. Time wore on and Puss was slyly introduced to the nursery of an evening when we youngsters were preparing our lessons, and at the sound of approaching
10 footsteps was carefully covered with an end of the rug, or under our dresses. Occasionally a faint mew was heard, and mamma would say, in either real or assumed indignation, "You have that horrid cat here." Of course everyone assumed an air and expression of surprise and innocence.

I was Pussy's particular favourite and friend, why or wherefore I know not; but she always seemed to come to me as if we both needed sympathy and protection. I was too delicate to go to school,
15 so my eldest sister acted as my teacher. I am sorry to confess that my ill-health had not a subduing influence on my general temper and character, and when mamma was from home my conduct towards my sister (teacher) was anything but respectful.

On the occasion to which I now allude, I had flatly and decidedly refused to sit down to my lessons. War was declared, and I ran into the garden, hotly pursued by my sister. When I entered
20 the garden, on looking to my right hand, Puss was the first object I saw, sitting by a wall. I was screaming at the pitch of my voice. When she saw my sister seize me, she, as it were, with one bound flew on my sister, yelling like a tigress, with her bristles erect and her body swollen to half its size again. I at once called her by every endearing term I could remember; I held out my hand for her.

At my voice the bristles fell down, the horrid yells gradually subdued to her usual soft purr; she
25 licked my hand, rubbed her head round my legs, and did everything in her power to show how delighted she was to see her friend all hale and sound. Strange, however, after that day, whenever she saw my sister, the angry howl and raising of the bristles began again. I could enumerate many more instances of her fidelity and sagacity, but none so wonderful as this, which, I think, rivals that of a dog.

1 This question is about **Source A**.

Read again the first part of **Source A** from line 1 to line 16.

Choose **four** statements below which are TRUE.

- Shade the boxes of the ones that you think are true.
- Choose a maximum of four statements.

A The writer has happy memories of pet cats. ☐

B He has always suffered from allergies. ☐

C His family preferred dogs to cats. ☐

D The writer thinks that cats are difficult to look after. ☐

E Stan used to follow the children. ☐

F Stan was much more active than he appeared. ☐

G Stan got on the bus with the children. ☐

H The writer seems anxious not to offend cat lovers. ☐

☐ 4 marks

Write your answers to questions **2**, **3** and **4** on separate pieces of paper.

2 You need to refer to both **Source A** and **Source B** for this question.

Use details from both sources. Write a summary of the differences between the two writers' attitudes towards their cats.

Use no more than two sides of A4 paper for your answer.

☐ 8 marks

3 For this question you need to refer only to **Source B** line 18 ('On the occasion') to the end of the text. How does the writer use language to express her feelings about both the cat and her sister?

Use no more than two sides of A4 paper for your answer.

☐ 12 marks

4 For this question you need to refer to **both** sources.

Both writers have written about the impact of cats on their lives, both positive and negative.

Compare how the writers convey this. In your answer you should:

- compare the different effects the cats have on the writers
- compare the methods the writers use to convey these effects
- support your answer with quotations from both texts.

Use no more than four sides of A4 for your answer.

☐ 16 marks

TOTAL

☐ 40

Mixed Test-Style Questions

Writing Task 1

Complete this writing task.

Allow yourself 45 minutes. Spend the first five minutes planning your work and the last five minutes checking your accuracy of spelling, punctuation and grammar.

Write your answer on a separate piece of paper.

You have been invited to enter a competition run by the International Photo Gallery; the winning entries will be posted on its website.

Write a description inspired by the photograph below.

Plan:

TOTAL

30

Writing Task 2

Complete this writing task.

Allow yourself 45 minutes. Spend the first five minutes planning your work and the last five minutes checking your accuracy of spelling, punctuation and grammar.

Write your answer on a separate piece of paper.

A national newspaper is running a creative writing competition based on the theme of relaxation. Write a description inspired by the photograph below.

Plan:

TOTAL

30

Mixed Test-Style Questions

Writing Task 3

Complete this writing task.

Allow yourself 45 minutes. Spend the first five minutes planning your work and the last five minutes checking your accuracy of spelling, punctuation and grammar.

Write your answer on a separate piece of paper.

Your local library is running a competition based on genres of fiction. Write the opening of either a detective story or a science fiction story.

Plan:

TOTAL

30

Writing Task 4

Complete this writing task.

Allow yourself 45 minutes. Spend the first five minutes planning your work and the last five minutes checking your accuracy of spelling, punctuation and grammar.

Write your answer on a separate piece of paper.

'Public transport should be free for all under-16s.' Write the text for a speech to be made in front of your local council, persuading them of this viewpoint.

Plan:

TOTAL

30

Writing Task 5

Complete this writing task.

Allow yourself 45 minutes. Spend the first five minutes planning your work and the last five minutes checking your accuracy of spelling, punctuation and grammar.

Write your answer on a separate piece of paper.

'What is your favourite sport or hobby?' Write an article for your school magazine, informing other students about one of your interests (e.g. gymnastics, football, playing the guitar, dancing).

Plan:

TOTAL

30

Writing Task 6

Complete this writing task.

Allow yourself 45 minutes. Spend the first five minutes planning your work and the last five minutes checking your accuracy of spelling, punctuation and grammar.

Write your answer on a separate piece of paper.

'The UK's age for voting should be lowered from 18 to 16.' Write an article for a national newspaper, providing a balanced argument about this issue.

Plan:

TOTAL

30

Mixed Test-Style Questions

Shakespeare: *A Midsummer Night's Dream*

Starting with this extract (Act 2 Scene 1, lines 188–204), analyse how Shakespeare presents Helena and Demetrius's relationship in the play.

Write your answer on a separate piece of paper.

DEMETRIUS

I love thee not, therefore pursue me not.
Where is Lysander and fair Hermia?
The one I'll slay, the other slayeth me.
Thou told'st me they were stolen unto this wood;
And here am I, and wode within this wood,
Because I cannot meet my Hermia.
Hence, get thee gone, and follow me no more.

HELENA

You draw me, you hard-hearted adamant;
But yet you draw not iron, for my heart
Is true as steel: leave you your power to draw,
And I shall have no power to follow you.

DEMETRIUS

Do I entice you? do I speak you fair?
Or, rather, do I not in plainest truth
Tell you, I do not, nor I cannot love you?

HELENA

And even for that do I love you the more.
I am your spaniel; and, Demetrius,
The more you beat me, I will fawn on you.

TOTAL

20

Shakespeare: *A Midsummer Night's Dream*

Starting with this extract (Act 5 Scene 1, lines 174–191), analyse how Shakespeare creates comedy in the play.

Write your answer on a separate piece of paper.

PYRAMUS
Thou wall, O wall, O sweet and lovely wall,
Show me thy chink, to blink through with mine eyne!

[Wall holds up his fingers]

Thanks, courteous wall: Jove shield thee well for this!
But what see I? No Thisbe do I see.
O wicked wall, through whom I see no bliss!
Cursed be thy stones for thus deceiving me!

THESEUS
The wall, methinks, being sensible, should curse again.

PYRAMUS
No, in truth, sir, he should not. 'Deceiving me'
is Thisbe's cue: she is to enter now, and I am to
spy her through the wall. You shall see, it will
fall pat as I told you. Yonder she comes.

[Enter Thisbe]

THISBE
O wall, full often hast thou heard my moans,
For parting my fair Pyramus and me!
My cherry lips have often kiss'd thy stones,
Thy stones with lime and hair knit up in thee.

PYRAMUS
I see a voice: now will I to the chink,
To spy and I can hear my Thisbe's face.

TOTAL

20

Shakespeare: *The Tempest*

Starting with this extract (Act 1 Scene 2, lines 242–257), analyse how Shakespeare presents Prospero's relationship with Ariel in the play.

Write your answer on a separate piece of paper.

ARIEL	Is there more toil? Since thou dost give me pains, Let me remember thee what thou hast promised, Which is not yet perform'd me.
PROSPERO	How now? moody? What is't thou canst demand?
ARIEL	My liberty.
PROSPERO	Before the time be out? no more!
ARIEL	I prithee, Remember I have done thee worthy service; Told thee no lies, made thee no mistakings, served Without or grudge or grumblings: thou didst promise To bate me a full year.
PROSPERO	Dost thou forget From what a torment I did free thee?
ARIEL	No.
PROSPERO	Thou dost, and think'st it much to tread the ooze Of the salt deep, To run upon the sharp wind of the north, To do me business in the veins o' the earth When it is baked with frost.
ARIEL	I do not, sir.
PROSPERO	Thou liest, malignant thing!

TOTAL

20

Shakespeare: *The Tempest*

Starting with this extract (Act 1 Scene 1, lines 198–217), analyse how Shakespeare presents the theme of magic in the play.

Write your answer on a separate piece of paper.

ARIEL	I flamed amazement: sometime I'd divide,
	And burn in many places; on the topmast,
	The yards and bowsprit, would I flame distinctly,
	Then meet and join. Jove's lightnings, the precursors
	O' the dreadful thunder-claps, more momentary
	And sight-outrunning were not; the fire and cracks
	Of sulphurous roaring the most mighty Neptune
	Seem to besiege and make his bold waves tremble,
	Yea, his dread trident shake.
PROSPERO	My brave spirit!
	Who was so firm, so constant, that this coil
	Would not infect his reason?
ARIEL	Not a soul
	But felt a fever of the mad and play'd
	Some tricks of desperation. All but mariners
	Plunged in the foaming brine and quit the vessel,
	Then all afire with me: the king's son, Ferdinand,
	With hair up-staring, – then like reeds, not hair, –
	Was the first man that leap'd; cried, 'Hell is empty
	And all the devils are here.'
PROSPERO	Why that's my spirit!
	But was not this nigh shore?
ARIEL	Close by, my master.
PROSPERO	But are they, Ariel, safe?

TOTAL

20

Answers

Assessment Table 1: Writing

Content	
8–10 marks	A fully convincing and effective response. Fully matched to audience and form. Fully matched to purpose. Extensive and ambitious vocabulary. Conscious crafting of language and sentence structures for effect throughout.
4–7 marks	A good, clear response. Mostly matched to audience and form. Mostly matched to purpose. Varied vocabulary. Clear attempts to craft language and sentence structures for effect.
1–3 marks	The response is generally focussed on the task set. Some match to audience and form. Some match to purpose. Some variation of vocabulary. Some attempts to craft language and/or sentence structures for effect.
Organisation	
8–10 marks	Writing is skilfully structured in order to effectively achieve its purpose. A range of interesting ideas are fully developed. Paragraphs are consistently used to separate ideas. A range of connectives are used appropriately and effectively.
4–7 marks	Writing is well-structured with a clear opening, middle, and ending. A number of ideas are included and most are developed. Paragraphs are mostly used appropriately. Some connectives are used to help show changes in focus.
1–3 marks	Some attempt to structure the writing as a whole. Limited ideas are included with some development. Some use of paragraphs to separate ideas. Limited use of connectives to show changes in focus.
Spelling, Punctuation and Grammar	
8–10 marks	High level of accuracy in spelling, including ambitious vocabulary. Full stops and capital letters are consistently accurate. A range of punctuation is used accurately within sentences. Tenses and sentence structures are securely controlled. A variety of sentence types are used for effect.
4–7 marks	Generally accurate spelling, including some complex and unfamiliar words. Full stops and capital letters are mostly accurate. Punctuation within sentences is mostly accurate. Tenses and sentence structures are usually controlled. There are attempts to use a variety of sentence types.
1–3 marks	Spelling of simple and familiar words is accurate. Some accuracy with full stops and capital letters. Limited use of accurate punctuation within sentences. Tenses and sentence structures are sometimes correct. Limited used of different sentence types.

Assessment Table 2: Reading and Shakespeare

Marks	Skills
16–20 marks	Your answer: • Evaluates the text critically • Shows perceptive understanding of the writer's methods • Selects a range of judicious detail from the text • Develops a convincing and critical response to the focus of the question.
11–15 marks	Your answer: • Clearly evaluates the effects on the reader • Shows clear understanding of the writer's methods • Selects a range of relevant detail from the text • Makes a clear and relevant response to the focus of the question.

6–10 marks	Your answer: • Makes some evaluative comments on effects on the reader • Shows some understanding of the writer's methods • Selects some appropriate references to the text • Makes some response to the focus of the question.
1–5 marks	Your answer: • Makes simple, limited comments on the effect on the reader • Shows limited understanding of the writer's methods • Selects simple references to the text • Makes a simple, limited attempt to respond to the focus of the question.

Assessment Table 3: Language and structure

Marks	Skills
7–8 marks	Your answer: • Shows perceptive understanding of the writer's use of language or structural features • Selects a range of judicious detail from the text • Makes sophisticated and accurate use of subject terminology.
5–6 marks	Your answer: • Explains clearly the effects of the writer's choices of language or structural features • Selects a range of relevant details from the text • Makes clear, relevant use of subject terminology.
3–4 marks	Your answer: • Attempts to comment on the effect of language or structural features. • Selects some appropriate details from the text • Makes some use of subject terminology.
1–2 marks	Your answer: • Makes one or two simple comments about language or structural features • Selects simple references to the text • Makes some simple use of subject terminology.

Pages 4–27 Reading

Pages 4–5

1. a) the most important or significant words or phrases **[1]**
   b) reading through quickly **[1]**
   c) putting into your own words **[1]**
   d) copying words directly from the text **[1]**
2. a) The Earl of Fosbury **[1]**
   b) rural Cheshire **[1]**
   c) in the 1860s **[1]**
   d) art and curiosities **[1]**
   e) in the grounds of the hall **[1]**
   f) every day during the summer **[1]**
   g) so that people can see how Sir Henry's family and servants lived and admire his collection **[1]**
   h) from making soap **[1]**
3. a), d), e) **[1]** for each correct answer **[3]**
4. a) 'wealthiest' **[1]**
   b) Sir Henry Morrison, his family and his servants **[1]**
   c) He collected art and curiosities. **[1]**
   d) 'every day during the summer' **[1]**
   e) 'altered' **[1]**
5. a) Quotation ✔ **[1]** b) Paraphrase ✔ **[1]**
   c) Paraphrase ✔ **[1]** d) Quotation ✔ **[1]**
   e) Quotation ✔ **[1]** f) Paraphrase ✔ **[1]**
6. Point **[1]** Evidence **[1]** Explanation (or Exploration) **[1]**
7. (P) The National Trust is busy improving the grounds/(E) where 'a major tree planting project is underway'./(E) The word 'major' suggests that there will be a lot of trees planted and 'underway' means that the work is continuing but no indication of when it will be completed is given. **[1]** for each correct answer. **[3]**

Pages 6–7

8 1939 **[1]**
9. Because she was 'always terrible at games'. **[1]**

10. 'stout' or 'grey-haired' **[2]**
11. a) 'severe' **[1]**
    b) 'the naughtiest girl in the school' **[1]**
12. The following are true: a), d), e) and h) **[1]** for each correct answer **[4]**
13. a) 'My jaw dropped.' **[1]**
    b) It means that her mouth opened. People sometimes open their mouths wide to express shock or surprise so this shows that May did not expect to see a house like Fosbury Hall. **[2]**

Pages 8–9

1. Infer – To understand something that is not directly stated.
   Deduce – To work something out from information you are given.
   Interpret – To explain the meaning of something.
   Imply – To suggest something without directly stating it. **[1]** for each correct answer **[4]**
2. a) ii and iv **[2]** b) i and iii **[2]** c) i and iv **[2]**
   d) i and iii **[2]**
3. a) Over fifty years **[1]** b) No **[1]** c) No **[1]**
   d) Three **[1]** e) No **[1]** f) Nobody **[1]**
   g) There are things in it that are worth a lot of money. **[1]** h) Sell them **[1]**
4. An example of a good answer is:
   The writer is very fond of her grandparents and enjoys their company. She 'used to love rummaging around' and 'poring over' photos with them. They seem to be very focused on the family, talking about the writer's mother and her brothers. They have been reluctant to get rid of things but have decided to have a 'giant clear-out' and make money, which suggests they have energy and are not over sentimental. Gran also shows she has a sense of humour, making a joke about people calling her 'tat' 'vintage'. **[1]** for each relevant point you have made supported by a reference to the text. **[3]**

Pages 10–11

5. romantic, detached, handsome, eccentric **[1]** for each correct answer **[4]**

6. The following are true: a), c), f) and h) **[1]** for each correct answer   **[4]**

7. a) He considered her special and precious, and perhaps spoiled her.   **[2]**
   b) They feel sorry for her.   **[1]**
   c) They did not really believe what he said.   **[1]**

8. An example of a good answer is:
   When she first met him Hannah 'was fascinated' by him. The focus on his 'soft black hair' and 'blue eyes' suggests that she is mainly attracted by his looks, although the use of the adjective 'vague' to describe his eyes implies that he might also be vague in his character. However, she enjoys his 'mist and glamour' for three years. Then things change and she starts to feel as if she is living with someone who is not really there: 'a fascinating spectre'.
   The birth of their daughter makes things worse and even the things that first attracted her become 'dreadful' to her. She feels even his 'flesh…did not seem like the flesh of a real man'. She even doubts his sanity, thinking that he might be 'a little bit mad'. **[1]** for each valid point you make and **[1]** for a relevant supporting quotation.   **[8]**

Pages 12–13

1. Paragraph – A section of a piece of prose.
   Stanza – A section of a poem, sometimes referred to as a 'verse'.
   Chronological order – Ordering events by time, from first to last.
   Flashback – Describing or narrating something that happened before the main action.
   Circular structure – Ending a text by returning to or referring back to the beginning. **[1]** for each correct answer   **[5]**

2. a change of time; a change of place; a change of topic; a new speaker. **[1]** for each correct answer   **[4]**

3. a) Agincourt 1415; First World War 1914–1918; Norman Conquest 1066; Second World War 1939–1945; Waterloo 1815.   **[1]**
   b) Norman Conquest 1066; Agincourt 1415; Waterloo 1815; First World War 1914–1918; Second World War 1939–1945.   **[1]**
   c) Second World War 1939–1945; First World War 1914–1918; Waterloo 1815; Agincourt 1415; Norman Conquest 1066.   **[1]**

4. a) 2 **[1]**   b) 4 **[1]**   c) 1 **[1]**   d) 3 **[1]**

5. <u>Despite</u> Sammy's best efforts, we all got back to school safely. <u>However</u>, that was not the end of the story. <u>The next day</u> we were all summoned to something called a 'special assembly'. <u>Basically</u> it was the headteacher ranting on about good behaviour, health and safety, the school's reputation and all the usual stuff.
   <u>Because</u> of what had gone on, we were told that we wouldn't be allowed on any more trips for the rest of the year. Some of the others were really upset and, of course, they all blamed Sammy. I was pleased. I hated school trips. <u>So</u> I decided to stay friends with Sammy after all. **[1]** for each correct answer   **[6]**

Pages 14–15

6. a) i) Your future – your choice   **[1]**
      ii) At the end of Year 9 you will have to choose your GCSE subjects. Here are some tips on how to do it.   **[1]**
   b) It expands on the headline and tells readers what the article is about.   **[2]**
   c) They help to organize the text into topics and guide readers through the information, pointing them towards areas of interest to them.   **[2]**

7. They give information in a list in a clear and simple way. **[2]**

8. They reflect questions that the writer thinks readers might want to ask and guide them to the answers below.   **[2]**

9. a) The writer tells readers what they should do when making their choice, giving alternative paths.   **[2]**
   b) The writer lists the subjects clearly in a table and tells readers how many they can choose from each column. **[2]**
   c) The writer outlines several factors to take into account when making the choice.   **[2]**
   d) The writer gives some ideas about where to go for help and includes a 'plug' for the school's options fair.   **[2]**

Pages 16–17

1. a) To talk in an unclear, usually quite quiet, way.   **[1]**
   b) To talk very quietly.   **[1]**
   c) To talk quickly, perhaps in an excited manner.   **[1]**
   d) To talk at length and earnestly, arguing a point.   **[1]**

2. a) personification **[1]**   b) simile **[1]**   c) onomatopoeia **[1]**
   d) alliteration **[1]**   e) assonance **[1]**   f) metaphor **[1]**

3. a) The writer wonders whether anyone will mark the deaths of people who have been slaughtered in an inhuman way (like animals), making you feel sorry for or angry about the way they are treated.   **[2]**
   b) The writer says that he is alone, using a comparison with a cloud to make it seem that he is wandering about aimlessly.   **[2]**

4. a) imperatives   **[1]**
   b) ellipsis   **[1]**
   c) exclamation mark   **[1]**
   d) present tense   **[1]**
   e) non-standard English   **[1]**
   f) first person; second person   **[2]**

5. a) list of three   **[1]**
   b) hyperbole (exaggeration)   **[1]**
   c) rhetorical question   **[1]**

6. a) By giving a variety of examples the speaker draws attention to how serious the situation is.   **[2]**
   b) The speaker exaggerates the effect of the pot holes to inspire emotion in the listeners.   **[2]**
   c) The speaker asks a rhetorical question to make the listeners think about where the responsibility lies.   **[2]**

Pages 18–19

7. a) The boy ✔   **[1]**
   b) He uses speech marks/inverted commas.   **[1]**

8. The word 'fiddle' is less formal than 'violin'. When the boy uses the word 'fiddle' he is showing by his informal tone his youth and spontaneous friendliness. It might also make both the prisoner and readers feel that he is going to play something happy, perhaps a folk tune or popular song, rather than a piece of classical music.   **[2]**

9. a) pitying   **[1]**
   b) smiled   **[1]**

10. Readers might wonder why he is in handcuffs. They might deduce that he has committed a crime, or at least is suspected of committing a crime, and is being taken to prison or maybe to court. His lack of freedom could inspire pity as it does in the boy or the thought that he is in handcuffs because he is dangerous might cause fear or worry. This could make the boy's attitude seem more surprising, as he might be expected to be frightened of the prisoner and avoid him.   **[4]**

11. He is singing about being free when he himself is clearly not free because he is handcuffed.   **[2]**

12. a) An oxymoron is two words put together, usually an adjective and a noun, that seem to be contradictory. **[1]**
    b) Readers might be amazed that someone in his situation could sing in a cheerful way. This might make them think that it is possible to have contradictory feelings at the same time and/or that human emotions are often complex.   **[2]**

13. The repetition of 'smiled' emphasises the unexpected mood that is created by the boy's offer. The use of the same word to describe the reactions of two men makes it seem that they are united although they might be expected to be

enemies, showing the power of the boy's innocence. The use of informal words such as 'fiddle' and 'twang' create an informal, fun atmosphere. This tone is added to by the use of short lines and rhyme when the prisoner sings. The oxymoron 'grimful glee' adds to the sense of surprise at the unusual situation. In the last four lines the pace slows with longer lines as the poet describes the situation and reflects on the scene. [1] for each correct point **[5]**

Pages 20–21

1. a) inform [1] b) persuade [1] c) instruct [1]
   d) entertain [1] e) describe [1] f) argue [1] g) advise [1]
2. 'chop'; 'place'; 'fry' [1] for each correct answer **[3]**
3. a) 'should': The purpose of the text is to advise readers not to respond to peer pressure. **[2]**
   b) 'would': The purpose of the text is to argue the writer's view on homework and to persuade others to abolish homework. **[2]**
   c) 'may': The purpose of the text is to persuade readers to increase their donations. **[2]**
4. a) The writer strongly expresses his/her opinion about the timetable changes and by asking a question seeks to persuade readers to change their mind. **[2]**
   b) The writer instructs readers about how to get to a place and then describes its attractions. **[2]**
5. a) This writer thinks that it is very important that people get inoculated against flu. The text begins by using impersonal, formal language that reflects the seriousness of the subject ('it is important') and the modal verb 'should' suggests that readers have an obligation to follow the advice. The second sentence uses the second person 'you' to involve the reader and the tone becomes less formal. The modal verb 'can' implies that people are being given an opportunity. **[3]**
   b) The text is in the first person, showing that it is about the writer's own opinion. The adverb 'strongly' shows the importance of the subject to the writer and the verb 'object' is also emotive. The second sentence uses the modal verb 'may' to create a gentler, more conciliatory tone as does the use of the verb 'suggest'. The question leaves the matter in the hands of the reader. **[3]**
   c) This writer uses the imperative 'continue' to give an instruction to readers. The order of the sentence, using the connective 'before' reflects the order in which things will happen. The second sentence has a different tone as the writer uses adjectives ('whitewashed' and 'azure') and a present participle ('glimmering') to convey the beauty of the scene to the reader and create a positive tone. **[3]**
6. Your reaction might be different from these examples. Any reasonable reaction will be rewarded.
   a) The text makes me feel that I should think about getting a flu jab and gives me the information I need, making it seem easy. **[1]**
   b) The text makes me realise that not everybody is happy with the changes. If I were the person addressed, I would seriously think about doing as the writer suggests. **[1]**
   c) The text makes me feel that I would be able to find the place easily, given the clear instructions, and it would be worth the walk and climb. **[1]**

Pages 22–23

7. 'Most of all, I have enjoyed meeting all of you.' **[1]**
8. a), d) and e) [1] for each correct answer **[3]**
9. Accept two from: 'How I got where I am today'; 'you can look it up on the internet'; 'my achievements' **[2]**
10. a) The tendency of people to portray themselves as victims.
    b) By using this phrase the speaker implies that she does not approve of people using their background or situation to gain sympathy.

c) Things that they say about themselves do not reflect the truth.
d) By using this phrase the speaker suggests that a lot of people make up things about themselves to make themselves look better or become more popular.
e) An inspiring person whose example should be followed.
f) By using this phrase the speaker expresses her admiration for her grandmother and suggests that she has tried to follow her example and be like her. She is also suggesting that her audience might aspire to be like her grandmother. **[6]**

11. a) Although she grew up when times were hard she did not complain but 'just got on with it', coping with problems and carrying on with normal life. She had a 'cheerful and optimistic' personality. She took care of her grandchildren and made them happy. She showed that being 'a good, caring person' was more important than fame or wealth. **[3]**
    b) She repeats her grandmother's phrase 'just got on with it', contrasting the down-to-earth, everyday tone of the phrase with the extraordinary events she describes. She uses the superlative 'most cheerful' to express how much she admires her. She gives a list of examples of things her grandmother did. She uses simple positive adjectives, such as 'good', 'caring' and 'secure' to paint an entirely positive picture of her grandmother. Finally, she adopts her grandmother's saying and uses it to directly address the audience. **[3]**

Pages 24–25

1. a), b), e), f) and h) **[5]**
2. a) Changing focus means moving from one thing to another. It could be a change of topic or character or scene. It could be moving from a general to a particular description or vice versa. It could be using a flashback. It could be moving between description, a character's inner thoughts, the narrator's comments and/or dialogue. **[3]**
   b) Any three from: flashback, dialogue, short/long paragraphs, sub-headings, circular structure. **[3]**
3. Ideas might include:
   • The use of the simple past verb 'quickened' to convey his mood as well as how he is walking.
   • The way the first sentence shares Mole's feelings with us, the adverb 'cheerfully' contrasting with the things he is trying not to imagine.
   • The repetition of 'another' showing how long the journey seems to be and emphasizing the fear the holes cause.
   • The use of dashes and exclamation marks in 'yes!-no!-yes!' to convey indecision and a state of excitement.
   • The change in vocabulary as Mole's fear increases, using emotive words like 'malice', 'evil' 'hard-eyed' and 'sharp'.
   • The writer uses the metaphor 'firing' to describe the 'evil glances' as if they were bullets putting him in physical danger.
   [1] for each valid point made and [1] for an appropriate supporting reference. **[8]**
4. Differences include:
   • In Source A the beach is crowded; in Source B it is quiet.
   • In Source A the children are playing together; in Source B they are isolated.
   • Source A focuses on children; Source B describes people of varying ages.
   • In Source A the writer in just observing the scene; in Source B the writer is involved.
   • In Source A the weather seems generally good with 'refreshing breezes'; in Source B it is described as 'miserable…cold, wet and windy'.
   • In Source A the writer does not mention anyone swimming or paddling in the sea; in Source B the writer describes a woman who has been swimming.
   [2] for each valid point made supported by reference to the text. **[8]**

5.	Examples of possible responses:

My impressions of King Alfred	Supporting quotation(s)
He was a good king in both peace and war	'As great and good in peace, as he was great and good in war'
He was interested in education and learning	'He loved to talk with clever men' 'He had studied Latin'
He was fair but could be strict	'He made just laws' 'punished…severely'
He cared about his people	'to do right to all his subjects'
He was patient and uncomplaining	'he bore it…like a brave good man'

How Dickens creates these impressions	Supporting quotation(s)
The first sentence introduces the king's character using repetition and alliteration to create an impact.	'great and good'
He gives an extensive list, using verbs in the past tense, of Alfred's achievements, starting each clause with 'he' to keep the focus on the king.	'He loved to talk…He had studied…He made just laws'
He uses a vivid image to convey the effect of Alfred's laws. The image also gives a sense of a rich, successful society.	'garlands of golden chains and jewels might have hung across the street'
He goes into great detail to explain how Alfred invented the 'lanthorn' to help him organise his time, showing his determination as well as his skill.	'And these were the first lanthorns ever made in England'
He uses a variety of adjectives with positive connotations to describe the king.	'good'; 'great'; 'brave'
He uses three comparative adjectives to summarise the effect of Alfred's reign on England.	'better, wiser, happier'

Use the table below to assess how well you have answered the question.

16–20 marks	Your answer: • Evaluates the text critically • Shows perceptive understanding of the writer's methods • Selects a range of judicious detail from the text • Develops a convincing and critical response to the focus of the statement.	You have included most of the points made above, supported with quotations. For a mark at the top of the range you will have made some original points of your own. You should have answered the question thoughtfully, stating clearly whether you think Dickens has made Alfred appear both heroic and human.
11–15 marks	Your answer: • Clearly evaluates the effects on the reader • Shows clear understanding of the writer's methods • Selects a range of relevant detail from the text • Makes a clear and relevant response to the focus of the statement.	You have included half or more of the points made above or valid points of your own, several of them about the writer's methods, mostly supported by reference to the text. You have given a clear answer to the question based on evidence.
6–10 marks	Your answer: • Makes some evaluative comments on effects on the reader • Shows some understanding of the writer's methods • Selects some appropriate references to the text • Makes some response to the focus of the statement.	You have included several of the points made above, including some that focus on the writer's methods. Some of your points are supported by quotations or other references to the text. You have included some personal responses to the statement.
1–5 marks	Your answer: • Makes simple, limited comments on the effect on the reader • Shows limited understanding of the writer's methods • Selects simple references to the text • Makes a simple, limited attempt to respond to the focus of the statement.	You have included two or three valid points with some reference to the writer's methods. You might have included one or two quotations or other references to the text. You have given some personal responses to the question.

Pages 28–31

1.	Any four from: whitewashed cottages; (the lights of) a public house; a church; a vicarage; a shop window/a sweet shop.	[4]

2.	The place is on 'Missel Moor' and moors are usually uninhabited and uncultivated places. Mrs Medlock also says it is five miles across the moor, which is a long way. In the third paragraph the scene changes from a busy village to countryside with 'hedges and trees' and then 'nothing different for a long time'. The loneliness of the place is reflected in the 'dense darkness' that surrounds them toward the end of the journey.	[4]

3.	a)	The focus is on Mrs Medlock and her instruction to Mary in answer to Mary's question.

	b)	The focus of the third paragraph is on a description of the changes that Mary notices during the journey.

	c)	This paragraph focuses on the last part of the journey, starting with the extra effort made by the horses.

	d)	The final paragraph is Mrs Medlock's speech, which brings us back to the question Mary asked in the first paragraph.	[4]

4.	a)	There are two stanzas of equal length, each one having four lines. The lines are of unequal length.	[1]

	b)	There is a regular rhyme scheme. The second and fourth lines of each stanza rhyme but the first and third do not (abcb).	[1]

	c)	In each stanza the first, second and fourth lines each have 3 stressed syllables. The first and second lines contain 5 syllables, the third contains 8, and the fourth contains 6. Every line contains 3 stressed syllables. The first two lines start on a stress and the fourth starts with an unstressed syllable. The third line also starts with an unstressed syllable.	[1]

5. 'Who has seen the wind?' makes readers think about how they experience the wind and what it means to feel something but not be able to see it. **[2]**

6. 'The trees bow down their heads': the trees bend over in the wind, giving the appearance of bowing down to a superior force. The phrase can also be considered pathetic fallacy as the feelings the poet gives to the trees reflect her own feelings. **[2]**

7. The writer is using the wind to describe experiences that are not physical, that nobody can see ('neither you nor I'). It is a spiritual force that people, like nature itself, should be in awe of, 'trembling' as they 'bow down their heads'. The powerful, invisible force can be equated with God. **[4]**

8. a), e) and f) **[3]**

9. a) 'which does not wish to incur additional unpopularity' **[1]**
   b) '(probably owing to higher wages)' **[1]**
   c) 'Several factors have made the refusal necessary.' or 'But the main cause is the lack of locomotives.' **[1]**

10. Ideas might include:
   - The writer of Source A writes about plans to reduce services while Source B talks of 'running more trips than ever'.
   - Source A is about trains, but Source B is about coaches.
   - Source A's plans are organized by the government ('the Ministry of Transport') while Source B is about the plans of a private company, 'Happy Days Travel'.
   - Source A says that 'no excursions will be provided at Easter or Whitsuntide' but Source B promises 'extra services laid on at times of peak demand such as Easter.'
   - Source B claims there is 'increased capacity and efficiency' whereas Source A bemoans the fact that 'we are still about 25 per cent below the pre-war standard'.
   [1] for each valid comparison made and **[1]** for each relevant quotation up to a maximum of **[8]**.

Pages 32–63 Writing

Pages 32–33

1. a) Purpose: inform; Audience: local adults; Form: local newspaper article **[3]**
   b) Purpose: persuade; Audience: school governors; Form: speech **[3]**
   c) Purpose: explain; Audience: children or teenagers; Form: leaflet **[3]**
   d) Purpose: argue; Audience: adults; Form: national newspaper article **[3]**

2. Ideas might include: an article will be in the third person and will not usually address the audience, while a speech will be in the first person and address the audience directly; an article may include more detailed complex information, while a speech may use more rhetorical techniques to directly engage the listener; an article may use subheadings and topic sentences to organise information, while a speech may use clear topic shifts and techniques of repetition to maintain clarity. **[1]** for each difference. **[4]**

3. Both audiences should be addressed formally. However, young and adult audiences may differ in the aspects of a topic that are of interest to them; they may also differ in the types of cultural and lifestyle references that they understand and can relate to. **[1]** for each similarity or difference. **[4]**

4. **[1]** for showing awareness of purpose, **[1]** for form and **[1]** audience; **[1]** for accurate spelling, punctuation and grammar. **[4]**

Pages 34–35

1. Time, place and focus. **[3]**

2. First paragraph break after: The few that had entered the house had never returned. //
   Second paragraph break after: The moon shone eerily across the overgrown garden, its ghostly light interrupting the drifting shadows. //
   Third paragraph break after: A dank, stale smell crept from the house and seemed to envelop her. // **[3]**

3. A new paragraph should be used each time Cathy enters a different part of the house or if any changes in time are signalled. **[1]** for each new paragraph. **[3]**

4. a) time: later, the next morning, the following evening
   b) sequence: second, next, finally
   c) cause and effect: because of this, as a result, due to
   d) compare: similarly, just as, in comparison
   e) contrast: however, on the other hand, whereas
   f) development: furthermore, in addition to this, moreover
   [1] per connective, maximum of **[18]**

5. **[1]** for identifying the correct type of connective and **[1]** for selecting a connective. For example:
   a) sequence (e.g. Next)
   b) contrast (e.g. However)
   c) cause and effect (e.g. because of)
   d) development (e.g. Furthermore) **[8]**

Pages 36–37

1. a) simple **[1]** b) complex **[1]** c) compound **[1]**
   d) compound **[1]** e) simple **[1]** f) complex **[1]**

2. a) Gradually turning to a golden brown colour, the cake began to rise. or The cake, gradually turning to a golden brown colour, began to rise. **[1]**
   b) Although old and threadbare, the armchair was incredibly comfortable. or The armchair was incredibly comfortable, although old and threadbare. **[1]**
   c) The boy, looking nervously at the clock, wrote hurriedly to finish the exam. or The boy wrote hurriedly to finish the exam, looking nervously at the clock. **[1]**

3. For example:
   a) Moving in time to the music, the girls danced. **[1]**
   b) The boy, scanning the shelves eagerly for food, found the fridge was empty. **[1]**
   c) Four cars raced down the road, their tyres screeching loudly. **[1]**

4. a) Present: I go / I am going;
      Past: I went / I was going / I had gone;
      Future: I will go / I will be going;
      Conditional: I would (should/might/could/ought to) go / I would have (should have/might have/could have/ought to have) gone. **[4]**
   b) Present: I listen / I am listening;
      Past: I listened / I was listening / I had listened;
      Future: I will listen / I will be listening;
      Conditional: I would listen / I would have listened. **[4]**
   c) Present: I make / I am making;
      Past: I made / I was making / I had made;
      Future: I will make / I will be making;
      Conditional: I would make / I would have made. **[4]**
   d) Present: I catch / I am catching;
      Past: I caught / I was catching / I had caught;
      Future: I will catch / I will be catching;
      Conditional: I would catch / I would have caught. **[4]**

5. It was Thursday and I was going to my friend's house. On the way, I bought some chocolate and a bottle of apple juice. The sun was shining and I felt in a really good mood. **[1]** for correcting each verb. **[5]**

6. I went to school yesterday but there was no one there. I walked around for quite a while, calling out to try and get someone's attention. I looked through the windows, and there was no one in any of the classes. It was scary being all alone in such a familiar place. Suddenly, with great embarrassment, I realised that it was Saturday. **[1]** for correcting each error. **[12]**

Pages 38–39

1. To show ownership or abbreviation/contraction/omission. **[2]**
2. a) The dog's bowl was empty. Or The dogs' bowl was empty. **[1]**
   b) I couldn't find the exit. **[1]**
   c) If they're going then so am I. **[1]**
   d) Joe's shirt was ripped. **[1]**

e) The three girls' clothes were covered in mud. [1]
f) I've got a headache. [1]

3.
a) Covered with a thick layer of cobwebs, the windows were impossible to see through. [1]
b) The roof, due to several missing tiles, let in water whenever it rained. [1]
c) The cupboards were full of jars, bottles, cans and tins. [1]
d) The wooden door was old and cracked, paint peeling from its rough surface. [1]

4. Harry followed his dog's paw prints through the snow, wondering what he would find. As he reached a tall tree, he saw his brother's shoe lying on the ground. Picking it up, Harry noticed blood on the shoe's leather. He dropped it in horror. The forest, full of shadows and strange sounds, seemed to close around him. [1] for correcting each error. [8]

5.
a) cats [1] b) mice [1] c) activities [1] d) boxes [1]
e) children [1] f) teeth [1] g) shelves [1]

6.
a) The horses were taken to the stable. [1]
b) Looking for some attention, the boy shouted and screamed. [1]
c) After the party, the kitchen looked horrendous. [1]
d) The plate smashed to pieces. [1]
e) The man threw the ball to his son. [1]
f) She bought six bars of chocolate from the shop. [1]
g) He asked her to wait by the door. [1]
h) The king had come to the end of his reign. [1]
i) The girls loved to go swimming. [1]
j) She slammed the window shut. [1]
k) A little happiness goes a long way. [1]
l) The woman had spent all her savings. [1]

7. Lucy's room was a mess. There were clothes, magazines, toys, and ornaments covering the floor. Looking around her, she didn't know where to start. She realised, staring at the overflowing cupboards and drawers, that she simply had too many things. She picked up an old pair of jeans, considering if she still needed them. Then she gathered up some discarded books and began to flick through them. She looked again at the chaos surrounding her. 'Would it be so bad just to leave it?' she wondered. [1] for correcting each error. [22]

Pages 40–41

1. Purpose: persuade; Audience: parents; Form: text for a leaflet [3]
2. [1] for each idea. Ideas might include: health, vitamins, 5-a-day, no harm to animals, better for the environment (less methane, more oxygen production), varied and balanced diet is easy to achieve, less processed food, organic, etc. [6]
3. [1] for each section idea, maximum [4]. Ideas might include: how varied and tasty vegetarian food is, the lack of cruelty to animals, the benefits to the environment, vegetarianism being a more sustainable diet for the future, ways to make the change, etc.
[1] for linking a technique to an idea, maximum [4]. Ideas for techniques might include: patterns of three, statistics, rhetorical questions, repetition, etc. [8]
4. [1] for clearly addressing parents; [1] for focussing on the topic of adopting a vegetarian lifestyle; [1] for summarising the areas that the leaflet will cover. [3]
5. [1] for establishing an idea through a topic sentence; [1] for dealing with the idea in a thorough way; [1] for using a persuasive technique. [3]
6. [1] for opening the paragraph with a connective phrase; [1] for using a topic sentence to establish the new focus; [1] for dealing with the idea in a thorough way; [1] for using a persuasive technique. [4]

Pages 42–45

1. Someone who tells a story. [1]
2. a) first person [1] b) unreliable [1] c) third person [1]
d) naive [1] e) intrusive [1]

3.
a) Argue, adults, article (in a national newspaper). [3]
b) Paragraphs [1]
c) Comparison, contrast, and cause and effect. [3]
4. [1] for an idea supporting the viewpoint and [1] for an idea opposing it. Ideas might include: play areas are safe as long as parents are vigilant; children need to expend energy for mental and physical health; it's important that all areas are safety tested and adhere to strict guidelines, etc. [2]
5. [1] for presenting a clear idea; [1] for starting the paragraph with a connective and topic sentence; maximum of [3] for accurate spelling, punctuation and grammar. [5]
6. An example of improved text:
There have recently been claims from different pressure groups that children's play areas should be closed down. It has been suggested that they pose a risk to children's safety. Although there are valid viewpoints on both sides, closing down such parks seems an extreme measure.
Play areas provide two vital functions in the lives of young people: they are a place to have fun and a place to socialise. While children must be kept safe, they must not spend their lives indoors and alone. Children develop by interacting with other children through acts of play, whether collaborative or competitive. Closing down areas that allow these activities would damage the lives of children across the nation. [10]
7. Any four from: a church; a churchyard; some homesteads; orchards; ornamental weathercocks; the rectory; trees; the road. [4]
8.
a) orchards are fields planted with fruit trees, the ones here surrounded by good walls. [1] This gives an impression of a place where people look after their properties and have plenty of produce. [1] [2]
b) the homesteads look grander than the rectory, where the minister or vicar lives. [1] The rectory is usually one of the biggest houses in a village so the 'homesteads' having 'more imposing fronts' gives the impression that there are quite a few wealthy people in the village. [1] [2]
c) People in the village have enough money to enjoy themselves, [1] suggesting that it is a prosperous place where at least some of the people do not have to worry about money. [1] [2]
9. The third person allows the writer to describe everything about Raveloe [1] and to comment on what she describes. [1] [2]
10. After giving a straightforward description of the village the writer begins to interpret what is being observed. She thinks the buildings 'showed at once the summits of its social life', interpreting the scene for readers rather than letting them come to their own conclusions. She then mentions 'the practised eye' implying that her knowledge of the world qualifies her to draw inferences about the village. There is an implied criticism of what she calls 'the several chiefs' when she juxtaposes a reference to the war with their 'rollicking' and 'jolly' lives. She is implying that they have made money out of the war. [4]
11. a) and d) [2]
12. Ideas might include:
• the comparison of the houses to the rectory, the houses being 'more imposing than' the place where the minister lives.
• the use of the word 'peeped', personifying the church as a rather shy unimportant person who stays in the background.
• the use of the adjective 'jolly' to describe the religious feasts of Christmas, Easter and Whitsun, suggesting the villagers are more interested in the non-religious celebrations that go with these feasts than in their religious significance. [4]
13. Ideas might include:
• She describes their 'homesteads' in some detail to convey their prosperity, using the adjectives 'large' 'well-walled', 'ornamental' and 'imposing', which together give a sense of security and wealth.

- She makes a negative observation – 'no great park and manor house' – to show that the farmers enjoy high status in the village, there being no-one who would be considered of higher status.
- The noun 'chiefs' shows that they think of themselves as leaders.
- 'At ease', 'rollicking' and 'jolly' convey a way of life which they are in control of and a sense that they are secure, perhaps even smug. **[4]**

Pages 46–47

1. **[1]** for each of: Facts, Opinions, Rhetorical questions, Emotive and empathetic language, Statistics, Triplets, Repetition, You (second person) **[8]**
2. **[1]** for identifying each technique. Washing your (You – second person) hands is the simplest thing (Opinion) you can do to remain healthy as it gets rid of bacteria (Fact). It reduces the chance of stomach-related illnesses by 60% (Statistic). All it takes is water, soap, and twenty seconds (Triplet). That's not difficult, is it? (Rhetorical question) This ensures that you aren't putting your health, and the health (Repetition) of your friends and family, at perilous risk. (Emotive and empathetic language). **[8]**
3. **[1]** for choosing a technique and justifying your choice.
4. **[1]** for using a technique in relation to handwashing.
5. **[1]** for each sentence that contains a persuasive technique related to your chosen product. **[4]**
6. **[1]** for identifying a topic; **[1]** for noting down 3 ideas about it or **[2]** marks for noting down 3 or more ideas about it. **[3]**
7. **[1]** for each sentence that uses a persuasive technique to encourage people to support your chosen topic. **[3]**

Pages 48–49

1. **[1]** for knowing that argue and persuade both require to present your views about an issue. **[1]** for realising that, with writing to argue, you need to provide a balanced viewpoint for and against. **[2]**
2. Any four from: facts, opinions, repetition, emotive and empathetic language, statistics, triplets. **[4]**
3. **[1]** for each idea, maximum **[18]**. For example, limiting mobile phone use may help young people connect with their families more but they may feel they're losing touch with their friends; closing a school at midday would give students more time to relax but it could mean they're missing out on their education.
4. **[1]** for each of: comparison, contrast, and cause and effect. **[1]** mark for each reason: connectives of comparison will link and develop the argument for; connectives of contrast will introduce the argument against and also allow counter-argument; connectives of cause and effect help to introduce explanations of justifications for your viewpoint. **[6]**
5. **[1]** for each topic sentence. For example: The first and most important reason for limiting young people's mobile phone use is to encourage them to reconnect with their families. **[6]**
6. **[1]** for a clear viewpoint; **[1]** for a clear explanation or justification of that viewpoint; **[1]** for using specific language technique to emphasise the argument (such as a triplet or a statistic); **[1]** for accurate spelling, punctuation and grammar. **[4]**

Pages 50–51

1. You are trying to get across your point of view about what someone should do and you are trying to encourage the reader to follow your advice. **[1]**
2. c) **[1]**
3. So the reader feels you are talking directly to them about their personal needs. **[1]**

4. **[1]** for declaratives (to show understanding and make general suggestions); **[1]** for imperatives (to give specific instructions). **[2]**
5. To provide the reader with clear steps to resolve their problem. **[1]**
6. **[1]** for each connective. For example: First, Next, Once this has been achieved, To build upon this, etc. **[4]**
7. Possibility and necessity **[2]**
8. **[1]** for each appropriate use of a modal verb. For example: You could make learning posters and put them on your walls. You must ensure you revise. You need to talk to your teacher about any areas you're unsure of. You ought to create a clear revision timetable. You should reshape your notes into cue cards so you can revise more efficiently. **[5]**
9. a) **[1]** for noting down up to 3 ideas; **[2]** for 4–6 ideas; **[3]** for 7+ ideas.
   b) **[1]** for clearly grouping your ideas.
   c) **[1]** for deciding which ideas are vital, quite important, or additional suggestions.
10. **[1]** for clearly conveying a piece of advice; **[1]** using a modal verb; **[1]** for using a declarative sentence; **[1]** for using an imperative sentence; **[1]** for using the second person; **[1]** for accurate spelling, punctuation and grammar. **[6]**

Pages 52–53

1. **[1]** for each synonym. For example:
   look: glance, peer, stare, observe, scrutinise
   say: whisper, reply, answer, shout, holler
   eat: nibble, gorge, stuff, devour, gobble
   want: yearn, need, require, desire, covet **[20]**
2. **[1]** for each synonym. For example:
   good: fine, great, amazing, wonderful, brilliant
   bad: unsatisfactory, disgusting, terrible, awful, horrendous
   big: large, massive, huge, enormous, colossal
   small: little, tiny, minute, miniscule, infinitesimal **[20]**
3. **[1]** for placing five words on a line of intensity.
4. **[1]** for each synonym used, maximum **[10]**. For example:
   I raced to the enormous party my friend was having; it was ear-splitting and riotous but I loved the music and the company.
   I wandered to the large party my friend was having; it was noisy and crowded but I enjoyed the music and the company.
5. **[1]** for each reason.
   a) short, simple sentences: emphasise a point; surprise your reader
   b) compound sentences: join two ideas; create a contrast
   c) complex sentences: build up a point; add extra detail
   d) lists: emphasise a point; build up a powerful image **[8]**
6. **[1]** for each sentence structure used. **[5]**

Pages 54–55

1. **[1]** for each suggestion, maximum **[3]**. For example, names of people and places, dates and times, statistics like costs or measurements, historical facts, etc.
2. chronological: the order in which things happen
   thematic: linking to themes or topics **[2]**
3. Time and place **[2]**
4. **[1]** for each answer in correct order

Famous people arrived in limousines.
They walked along the red carpet to the film premiere.
They had their photographs taken outside the doors to the cinema.
Champagne and canapes were served before the film.
Everyone watched the film.
There was applause because everyone enjoyed the film.
All the celebrities went to an after-show party

[7]

5. Examples of appropriate connective words and phrases include: At the start of the night; Once they had arrived; At the end of the red carpet; In the foyer; At 7 p.m.; As the credits rolled; After the premiere. **[1]** for each suitable connective. **[7]**
6. a) chronological **[1]**
   b) thematic **[1]**
7. **[1]** for each set of ideas, maximum **[4]**. Sets of information might include details about: what the charity raises money for; the charity's current projects; the history of the charity; how you got involved in the charity; other ways people can get involved; celebrities who are involved in the charity.
8. **[1]** for focussing on one set of information; **[1]** for using some factual information; **[1]** for incorporating a connective of time or place; **[1]** for accurate spelling, punctuation and grammar. **[4]**

Pages 56–57

1. Writing to explain requires more detail about the causes and effects of a topic. **[1]**
2. a) Explain – it requires explanation of the effects of smoking. **[1]**
   b) Inform – it requires a chronological account of what happened. **[1]**
3. Effect: a), b), d)   Cause: c), e), f) **[6]**
4. **[1]** for each connective. For example: as a result, consequently, due to, because of this, therefore. **[5]**
5. Present tense to explain a current issue **[1]**; past tense to explain how something happened **[1]**.
6. Paragraphs help to clearly separate your different ideas **[1]**; topic sentences clearly establish a new idea **[1]**.
7. **[1]** for each idea and **[1]** for a cause, effect or piece of evidence. Ideas might include:
   Literacy – better vocabulary, better comprehension, do better in all school subjects
   Relaxation – time spent alone and quiet, lose yourself in a book, purely for enjoyment
   Mental stimulation – books make young people think, escape passive technology, imagination **[6]**
8. **[1]** for establishing a clear idea with a topic sentence; **[1]** for using a connective of cause or effect; **[1]** for using an example or fact as evidence; **[1]** for accurate spelling, punctuation and grammar. **[4]**

Pages 58–59

1. A simile is a comparison that uses 'like' or 'as' **[1]**; a metaphor is a comparison that is written as if it's true **[1]**.
2. For example: The fear made my legs feel like stone. *or* It was like my legs had turned to stone. **[1]**
3. For example: Her words were arrows fired at my heart. **[1]**
4. Personification is writing about an object or idea as if it has human qualities. **[1]**
5. **[1]** for a simile, **[1]** for a metaphor and **[1]** for some personification.
6. Sight, sound, smell, touch, taste. **[5]**
7. **[1]** for each sense used. **[5]**
8. **[1]** for each of alliteration, sibilance, onomatopoeia or assonance. **[3]**
9. **[1]** for each of use of alliteration, sibilance, onomatopoeia or assonance. **[3]**
10. **[1]** for each group of ideas. For example: the beach – waves, sand, palm trees, empty; the jungle – thick foliage, huge trees and flowers, strange birds and animals; a waterfall – jagged rocks, rushing water, noise and danger; a cave behind the waterfall – dark and shadows, damp, echoes and strange smell. **[4]**
11. **[1]** for using a variety of verbs, adjectives and adverbs; **[1]** for each use of descriptive techniques, maximum **[3]**; **[1]** for accurate spelling, punctuation and grammar. **[5]**

Pages 60–63

1. a) purpose: describe; audience: adults; form: creative writing/description/story (in a national newspaper). **[3]**
   b) simile, metaphor, personification **[3]**
   c) sight, sound, smell, touch, taste **[5]**
2. **[1]** for additional ideas to focus on during the description, maximum **[2]**. Ideas might include: the sand; the desert stretching into the distance; feeling scared, lost, or thirsty; vultures flying above, etc.
3. Drifting awake, I opened my eyes. A blinding light hit me like burning arrows and I quickly snapped my eyelids shut again. Gradually, I peeked through my lashes to see the bright sun overhead: a ball of fire hanging in a clear blue sky. Its rays were fierce against my face and already I could feel my skin becoming uncomfortable. The heat seemed to prickle my flesh like red-hot needles. Raising my trembling hands to shield my eyes from the sun, I began to look around to work out where I was. **[10]**
4. **[1]** for clearly shifting the focus of the description; **[1]** for using imagery or one of the senses; maximum **[3]** for accurate spelling, punctuation and grammar. **[5]**
5. Mark your answer using Assessment Table 1, given on p102. **[30]**
6. Source A: a), c), f), g)   Source B: b), d), e) **[7]**
7. Ideas might include:
   - The use of positive-sounding adjectives such as 'diverse', 'exciting' and 'vibrant'.
   - Fashionable contemporary vocabulary including the words above as well as 'upmarket', 'shabby chic' and 'vintage outlets', showing the place is up to date and appealing to younger readers.
   - Use of the second person, 'you', directly addressing readers and the first person 'I', making the text more personal as though the writer is chatting with the readers.
   - The use of lists in long sentences to emphasise both the number and variety of attractions.
   - The use of elisions in 'you'll' and 'there's', as well as slang such as 'buzzing', helping to create an informal tone.
   - Short, simple sentences used for emphasis and to contrast with the long lists: 'You'll be spoilt for choice.'
   - Repetition in 'again and again'. **[8]**
8. Ideas might include:
   - The use of the first person indicating that this is a personal memory ('we' and 'I'), and that the writer is giving personal opinions.
   - Phrases such as 'our mum', 'messages', 'that little bit closer' and 'more or less' creating an informal, cosy tone.
   - The use of the second person 'you' to mean 'one' or 'anyone', including the reader.
   - The use of quotation marks in 'classier' and upmarket' to suggest that these are not words the writer would normally use and introduces a slightly ironic tone.
   - The use of a long list of shops to emphasise the number and variety of shops.
   - The use of the old-fashioned names for types of shops ('fishmonger'; 'chandler'; 'greengrocer') with which younger readers might not be familiar, showing how much shopping has changed.
   - Elisions combined with colloquial language to create a chatty tone: 'Still, I'm'. **[8]**
9. Ideas might include:
   - Source A mentions people travelling a distance to get there ('easily accessible') whereas it is described in Source B as a local shopping street ('closer and safer').
   - Source B describes a lot of restaurants and bars while Source B mentions only 'two pubs'.
   - The shops in Source A sell things like 'trinkets', books and antiques, which people buy for pleasure whereas Source B's shops are focused on daily necessities ('anything you needed').

- Source A emphasizes that the lane is 'positively buzzing' at night as well as in the day but Source B is about shopping during the day.
- Source A suggests that people go to Oak Lane to try new experiences, such as different styles of restaurant. Source B talks about its familiarity: 'long-established'; 'The shopkeepers knew us and we knew them.' **[8]**

10. a) purpose: persuade; audience: adults/radio listeners; form: speech **[3]**
    b) Pretend you *do* agree with the statement. **[1]**
    c) Facts, opinions, repetition, empathy and exaggeration, statistics, triplets, rhetorical questions, you/second person. **[8]**

11. [1] for each idea that would persuade people to support the statement. **[2]**

12. [1] for each persuasive technique used, maximum **[3]**. Possible changes might include: The main reason fast food should be banned is that it is unhealthy. It is full of things that are bad for your body: sugar, salt and saturated fat. Do you really want an excess of that in your body or the bodies of your children? These things can affect your weight and increase the risk of different diseases, such as diabetes, heart problems and some cancers. Even items that we think are healthy can be worse than expected. For example, salads are often accompanied by dressings that are high in calories while some fruit juices contain a lot of sugar. It is imperative that we ban fast food in order to create a healthier nation.

13. [1] for presenting a clear idea; [1] for using a persuasive technique; [1] for accurate spelling, punctuation and grammar, maximum **[3]**.

14. Mark your answer using Assessment Table 1, given on p102. **[30]**

Pages 64–79 Shakespeare

Pages 64–65

1. a) Hermia and Lysander are in love with each other, despite her father's disapproval. **[1]**
   b) Demetrius is in love with Hermia but she doesn't return his love. **[1]**
   c) Helena is in love with Demetrius but he doesn't return her love. **[1]**

2. Egeus believes Lysander has tricked Hermia into loving him; he wants her to marry Demetrius or be executed. **[1]**

3. Theseus decides that Hermia must marry Demetrius otherwise face being sent to a nunnery or execution. **[1]**

4. Hermia and Lysander plan to escape Athens to his aunt's house and then get married. **[1]**

5. Hermia confides in Helena as she is her best friend but Helena tells Demetrius, hoping he will love her for it; Demetrius leaves in pursuit of Hermia and Lysander, and Helena follows. **[2]**

6. a) Quince and Bottom are friends; although Quince is the leader (or director) of the actors, Bottom keeps trying to take control. **[1]**
   b) Oberon and Titania are King and Queen of the fairies but they have fallen out over a child: Titania wants to look after the boy and keep him as a companion but Oberon is jealous and wants the boy to be his knight. **[1]**

7. The Mechanicals go to the forest to practise their play in private. **[1]**

8. Oberon tells Puck to collect a magical love potion; they place it on Titania then transform Bottom's head into that of an ass and watch as the pair fall in love. **[1]**

9. Oberon tells Puck to put a love spell on Demetrius so he falls in love with Helena but he puts the potion on Lysander. **[2]**

10. Lysander falls in Love with Helena instead of Hermia; Puck also puts the potion on Demetrius so both men fall in love with Helena; eventually he removes the spell from Lysander. **[2]**

11. Lysander and Hermia, and Demetrius and Helena are in love so Theseus decides that they should get married at the same time as he marries Hippolyta; the Mechanicals perform their play at the wedding and are congratulated; Oberon and Titania are reconciled. **[3]**

Pages 66–67

1. Demetrius's love for Hermia can be seen in his use of the adjective 'sweet', while the verb 'relent' could suggest his desperation to be with her. However, the phrase 'certain right' also shows he feels Hermia has to love him (because her father agrees) and the verb 'yield' suggests he sees love as a contest. **[2]**

2. Hermia's use of contrasts (the abstract nouns 'curses' and 'love') show her frustration at being loved by someone she doesn't love back. Helena's exclamation shows her own frustration that she wants Demetrius's love while Hermia does not. The reference to prayers shows she worships him and is desperate for his love. **[2]**

3. The list of violent verbs shows how Helena is desperate and how she is demeaned by her feelings of unrequited love. This is emphasised by her comparing herself to a dog, describing herself using the adjective 'unworthy', and asking his permission ('give me leave') as if she is his servant. **[3]**

4. Lysander's metaphors suggest that his love for Hermia is so strong they will never be parted (the verb 'knit') and that he sees them both as one person ('one heart'). The images of union could also be interpreted as his wish to make love to her. The phrase 'interchanged with an oath' shows his faithfulness and relates to the promises made in marriage. **[3]**

5. The list of positive adjectives is used to show Demetrius's new love for Helena; the choice of words suggests he now worships her and this is emphasised by his exclamation. His language sounds like romantic poetry (reminiscent of images in Shakespeare's earlier Sonnet 18) rather than his previous cruelty: he compares her lips to ripe cherries to suggest he wants to kiss her and says her eyes are beautiful (in comparison to them, crystal appears dirty). However, Helena, who has been desperate for his love, thinks it is just a trick ('spite', 'merriment'). Her rejection of his love is shown through imagery that contrasts with Demetrius's words (using 'Hell' compared to his use of 'goddess'). **[4]**

6. In Act 1, Lysander's adjective 'gentle' and Hermia's adjective 'good' show their love, care and respect for each other. However, in Act 3, he uses the insulting adjectives 'vile' and 'loathed' as well as the serpent simile and the poison metaphor to show that he hates her; her love for him is still the same 'Sweet love' and her surprise at his cruelty is shown through her questioning and the use of the adjective 'rude'. In Act 1, the reference to 'a morn of May' shows they have spent romantic times together but, in Act 3, his sneer 'thy love?' and her reference to 'change' shows how their relationship has altered. The verbs 'marry' and 'swear' in Act 1 suggest their love and faithfulness; this is emphasised by her classical references to Cupid and Venus. In contrast, Lysander calling Hermia a 'cat' and a 'burr' in Act 3 suggests he finds her faithfulness annoying; this is emphasised by the word 'hence' and his repeated imperative 'out' to show that he doesn't want her near him. Their sharing of the iambic pentameter in Act 1 is used to represent their love and unity but, in Act 3, this is presented as Lysander interrupting her and attempting to cut off any romance. **[6]**

Pages 68–69

1. The verbs 'jest' and 'smile' indicate that Puck and Oberon have a relaxed and friendly relationship, although Puck's role in these actions suggest he has less status than Oberon and wishes to please him; their relationship

is based around the idea of a king and his fool. This is emphasised by the respect he shows when he refers to Oberon as 'my lord' and uses the contrasting noun 'servant' to describe himself. [2]

2. The insulting adjectives ('proud', 'jealous', and 'rash') show that Titania and Oberon are in conflict with each other. The phrase 'Ill met' indicates that Oberon is not pleased to see her; similarly she points out that she has decided not to spend any time with him ('forsworn his bed and company'). However, when Oberon uses the verb 'tarry' (meaning to stay), it suggests he would like to resolve their conflict. His reminder that he is her 'Lord' could be a reference to their previous love or it could be a suggestion that he feels she should obey him. [3]

3. Shakespeare creates humour because Titania's language does not match the scene on stage: Bottom with a donkey's head. She calls him an 'angel' and uses the romantic image of a 'flowery bed' to suggest her love for him. Shakespeare employs irony to create humour when Titania says Bottom is 'as wise' as he is 'beautiful': the love potion affects her perspective whereas the audience see the donkey-headed Bottom as foolish and ugly. [2]

4. The adverb 'straightway' suggests their enjoyment of the potion's power and this is emphasised by how the humorous rhyming of 'pass' and 'ass' highlights Titania's embarrassing situation. Oberon's pleasure is shown in his admission that the trick has worked 'better' that he expected. [2]

5. Puck addresses the audience directly ('you'). Referring humorously to the title of the play, he asks them to imagine they have slept ('slumbered') and that the play has actually just been a dream ('these visions'). In a way, this makes the play seem more real because it hasn't been 'acted' but instead 'imagined' by the audience. [2]

6. Shakespeare uses personification to suggest that their conflict has disturbed nature. Nature is described as angry ('in revenge') and diseased ('contagious fogs'). The elements of air ('wind'), water ('sea') and earth ('land') seem in conflict with each other and this has created heavy floods ('overborne their continents'), representing how Oberon and Titania have broken out of their normal, harmonious relationship. This lack of normality is also described through the image of the seasons changing, with winter (representing the unhappiness of their disagreement, or the coolness of their feelings towards each other) appearing when it should be summer (representing love, which is emphasised by the romantic image of the 'crimson rose'). [4]

7. In Act 2, Oberon gives Titania orders (the imperative 'Give me'), although this could be seen as bargaining with her to try to resolve their conflict, while she challenges his status by belittling the worth of his 'fairy kingdom'. However, in Act 4 they show mutual love and respect through their use of the titles 'my queen' and 'my lord'. Their conflict is shown in Act 2 through her awareness that they will argue angrily (the verb 'chide') and her leaving the stage suggests she thinks their problem cannot be resolved. In comparison, Act 4 shows them magically travelling around the world together ('We the globe can compass' and 'our flight'), and her mirroring of his words also suggests their unity. In a brief soliloquy in Act 2, Oberon suggests his frustration with Titania ('go thy way'); his feeling that she has insulted him ('this injury') shows he blames her for the conflict and cannot see her viewpoint. The powerful verb 'torment' emphasises the damage to their relationship by showing his desire for revenge. However, Oberon's reference in Act 4 to the end of the night ('Trip we after night's shade') could symbolise the end of their argument, and Titania's wish for an explanation of the night's events may suggest a willingness to put the argument behind her. [6]

Pages 70–71

1. Quince creates comedy through the way his words don't make sense, 'wedding day at night' and 'lamentable comedy'. These oxymorons make Quince sound foolish. [2]

2. Flute creates comedy through his embarrassment about playing the female role (linking to the contexts of the Elizabethan era when all female roles were played by men). His phrase 'I have a beard coming' could be comic because of how unfeminine he will look or because he's desperately trying to prove he's too masculine for the role. [2]

3. Comedy is created through Bottom's wish to play every role ('play Thisbe too') and the ridiculous image of this when he changes his voice to show how he would swap between the two roles of Pyramus and Thisbe. More comedy is created through characters appearing foolish by using the wrong words when Bottom describes his 'monstrous little voice'. Comedy is also created through the conflict between Quince being in charge and Bottom wanting to take over. [3]

4. Shakespeare creates comedy by having Bottom late to appear ('Your cue is past'), making his entrance with the ass's head more dramatic. The romantic scenario of the play they are performing also contrasts humorously with Bottom's monstrous appearance. Bottom performs his lines with punctuation in the wrong place (saying 'If I were fair, Thisbe' instead of 'If I were, fair Thisbe'); as well as making him sound like a bad actor, it creates irony by describing himself as fair despite him having an ass's head. The panic created on stage ('Fly, masters! Help!') should come across as farcical rather than frightening. [3]

5. Quince's performance creates comedy because Shakespeare has deliberately mis-punctuated the speech to change its meaning. This makes Quince sound foolish but also sounds as if he is being rude ('If we offend, it is with our good will.'). The double meaning of 'end' is also used to create an oxymoron that makes Quince sound foolish, 'beginning of our end'. Comedy is also created through the reaction of the stage audience, with Theseus joking that Quince ignores the punctuation in his lines and Lysander continuing this joke through his simile about a horse that cannot be stopped. [4]

6. In Act 3, Bottom is presented as a bad actor because he misreads his words ('odious') and creates an unromantic phrase that contrasts with the romantic play they are performing. However, in Act 5, he performs his speech correctly and the mood is moving rather than ridiculous ('Quail, crush, conclude, and quell.'). His poor acting is emphasised in Act 3 by the way Quince sounds exasperated when he corrects him, 'Odorous!', but in Act 5 Bottom's acting is good enough to move Hippolyta ('Beshrew my heart'). Bottom's acting is mocked in Act 3 by Puck who describes it as 'stranger' than any he's seen before whereas, in Act 5, Theseus takes his performance seriously and praises his acting ('This passion'). [6]

Pages 72–73

1. a) Prospero saved Ariel from Sycorax and made him his servant. Prospero treats Ariel kindly but can be threatening. Ariel is respectful but wants the freedom that Prospero has promised him. [1]
   b) Prospero was initially kind to Caliban and tried to educate him but he tried to attack Miranda. Now, Prospero treats him harshly and uses him as his slave. [1]
   c) Prospero loves and protects Miranda, his daughter, but he also controls her using magic. [1]
   d) Antonio is Prospero's brother; with the help of Alonso, he betrayed Prospero by stealing the Dukedom. [1]
   e) Gonzalo was once a trusted servant to Prospero; he helped Prospero and Miranda to escape Milan when Antonio seized power. [1]

2. The shipwreck seems like revenge but Prospero has a more complex plan for the men to accept how they wronged him and for all the characters to make amends. [1]

3. They plan to kill the other two men while they are sleeping. [1]

4. Trinculo and Stephano are friends from the ship; they are amused by Caliban and the three get drunk together then hatch a plan to kill Prospero. [1]

5. He is testing Ferdinand to see whether he is worthy of Miranda. [1]
6. He has them chased by magical hell hounds. [1]
7. Forgiveness, although he is still critical of Antonio and Sebastian for being untrustworthy. [1]
8. He gives him his freedom. [1]
9. Alonso returns the dukedom to Prospero; Prospero reveals that Ferdinand is alive and in love with Miranda. [1]

Pages 74–75

1. He questions/interrogates Ariel. The verb 'bade' shows he gives orders to Ariel. The phrase 'to the point' shows he expects his orders to be completed perfectly. [2]
2. 'Hag-seed' shows he is free to insult Caliban. The different imperative verb phrases show he can give Caliban orders. The word 'fuel' shows Caliban is a servant doing manual labour. [2]
3. The verb phrase 'must obey' shows he does not want to follow Prospero's orders but has no choice. The references to Prospero's 'art' and 'power' suggest he is scared of Prospero, and this is emphasised by the suggestion that he's stronger than a god. The fact that this is an 'aside' could also suggest he does not want Prospero to know the extent of his fears. [3]
4. The repetition of 'hail', and the use of 'master' and 'sir' suggest Ariel has great respect for Prospero. The noun 'pleasure' shows he wants to please Prospero. However, the adjectives 'great' and 'grave', as well as the reference to his orders ('answer') could suggest he is scared of Prospero and feels he has to obey and flatter him (in order to gain his freedom). [3]
5. Prospero's dislike and disgust of Caliban can be seen in his insults. He is also disappointed in his failure to tame/educate Caliban ('nature/nurture', 'all lost'). The metaphor 'his mind cankers' suggests he is perhaps worried that Caliban is getting worse as he gets older. He wants to punish ('plague') Caliban for plotting against him. Caliban's hatred of Prospero is implied by the plot to kill him. He is clearly eager to kill Prospero but scared of being found out (the phrases 'pray you' and 'tread softly'). [4]
6. In the first extract, Prospero threatens Ariel to make him comply ('till thou hast howled'), whereas he is pleased with him in the second extract (the adjective 'dainty'). Whereas he shows his ability to control Ariel ('peg thee') in the first extract, he promises him his freedom in the second extract. Ariel seems less frightened of Prospero in the second extract because instead of fearfully apologising ('Pardon master') he is happily singing to him ('Merrily'). However, both extracts show how Prospero controls Ariel: saying he will follow any 'command' given by Prospero and the imperative 'to the King's ship'. [6]

Page 76

1. She is impressed and thinks he is a god (the adjectives 'noble' and 'divine'); she is curious ('thing') because she has never seen a man before. [2]
2. He appears satisfied or pleased that they are in love (the 'powers' metaphor) and the noun 'prize' suggests he hopes they are a good match for each other. However, he is cautious and feels it is his fatherly duty ('must') to test their love (the adjective 'uneasy'). He worries that such a quick ('swift') romance won't lead to a lasting, deep affection (the repetition of 'light'). The secretive [aside] and the word 'business' also remind us that Prospero is arranging this relationship without either knowing. [3]
3. Romantic and respectful noun phrases ('dear mistress' and 'precious creature') show that Ferdinand is falling in love with Miranda and wants to treat her well. His hyperbole ('crack my sinews, break my back') show his wish to prove his love and respect for her and this is emphasised by his reference to 'dishonour'. Her willingness to break her father's rules and help Ferdinand show Miranda's love.

Her repetition of verb phrases ('I'll bear... I'll carry') also show a wish to prove her love; the words may also be a reference to her wish to marry him and bear/carry his child. Shakespeare also emphasises the romantic union between Ferdinand and Miranda by having them share the iambic pentameter. [4]

Page 77

1. His positive words like 'merry' show he is trying to get Alonso to see the best of things; the contrast between 'loss' and 'escape' suggests that the shipwreck could have been worse as they all could have died: his 'joy' comes from the fact he is still alive. [2]
2. Alonso shows despair, grief, and hopelessness. The personification of 'hope' is used to show that he is giving up on finding his son and this is emphasised by the short sentence 'Well, let him go'. He accepts that his son is 'drowned' and the word 'stray' suggests he realises that their search for him has been pointless. When he personifies the sea as mocking them, it could imply frustration in his inability to rescue his son. [3]
3. Prospero's friendly ('embrace' and 'hearty welcome') and respectful ('sir King') speech shows how he has forgiven Alonso's mistreatment of him. However, he does remind him of this mistreatment in the adjective 'wronged'. He also appears to be trying to seem powerful in front of Alonso and perhaps intimidate him: the verb 'behold' sounds grand, like a magician showing off a trick, and the exclamation mark suggests the actor playing Prospero should raise his voice to sound impressive. Alonso appears contrite ('pardon me' and returning the dukedom to Prospero) and begging for forgiveness ('entreat') suggests he is sincere, as well as implying he may be scared of Prospero. His question suggests he is astonished and intrigued by Prospero's survival. [4]

Pages 78–79

1. Ariel's verb phrases display his magical abilities; the reference to water, fire, and air imply his magical power are linked to having power over the elements; the image of riding on the clouds makes him sound formless. [2]
2. Prospero doesn't doubt his magical powers ('be sure') and uses them to enslave Caliban and make him behave in a certain way ('For this'); this is emphasised by his threatening tone ('tonight thou shalt have'). The nouns 'cramps' and 'side stitches' describe pain, suggesting that magic can be a form of cruelty. [2]
3. Sebastian says he will copy Antonio's past behaviour ('thy case [...] my precedent') showing he is being corrupted by Antonio; corruption is linked to a desire for wealth and power, through the verb phrases 'thou got'st' and 'I'll come by'. The reference to 'thy sword' shows that corruption is linked to violence; its immorality is emphasised by the fact that Sebastian is planning to kill his own brother. [3]
4. The use of '[aside]' shows corruption through Antonio and Sebastian's secret plotting; corruption is shown to be evil by the way they plan to take 'advantage' of Alonso and Gonzalo's tiredness ('oppressed with travail'), in order to attack them when they are most vulnerable ('cannot use such vigilance'). The phrases 'next' and 'let it be tonight' suggest their corruption because they appear eager to kill their companions in order to gain power. [3]
5. Magical powers appear frightening (the adjective 'dread') and powerful (the verbs 'rifted', 'shake', and 'pluck'd'). The nouns also show that Prospero's magical powers are focussed on the control of nature: thunder, fire, oak, bolt. Prospero acknowledges the violent nature of his magic when he describes it using the adjective 'rough'. His decision to give up ('abjure') his magic suggests it has served its purpose and he does not need it anymore; it could also imply that he sees it is as wrong. The unnatural aspect of his magic is highlighted when he mentions

his ability to bring the dead back to life ('waked their sleepers'). **[4]**

6. Ariel and Prospero both present corruption as something evil: Ariel uses the word 'sin' while Prospero describes Antonio as 'unnatural'; Prospero also links it to the sin of greed by describing Antonio's 'ambition'. Corruption is presented as deserving punishment, with Ariel personifying 'Destiny' as causing the men's downfall and Prospero using the metaphor 'inward pinches' to describe the guilt Sebastian feels for plotting against his brother. While Ariel suggests corrupt people should be shown no forgiveness ('most unfit to live'), Prospero presents people as deserving of mercy if they show contrition for their corruption, 'I do forgive thee'. **[6]**

Pages 80–85

1. a) purpose: inform; audience: over 60s; form: guide **[3]**
   b) facts **[1]**
   c) thematically (because it's about a topic rather than an event that has happened) **[1]**
2. **[1]** for each idea that would inform the over 60s about social media. **[2]**
3. **[1]** for adding a topic sentence to each paragraph, maximum **[2]**. **[1]** for removing the opinions. Possible changes might include:
   To help you access social media, there are lots of words and phrases it is useful to know. One that you will see a lot is ~~My favourite social media word is obviously going to be~~ 'like'. This is the way in which you show approval for something that has been posted. ~~It's a great feeling when someone likes something you have done.~~ **It's polite to 'like' posts by friends and relatives. Another key word is** ~~The best things to like are other people's~~ 'selfies'. If you have never heard this term, it's when you take a photograph of yourself doing something fun or interesting. ~~Taking selfies is so much fun.~~
   There are many benefits of social media to the over 60s. One benefit of social media is that you can keep in touch with people all the time. ~~This is wonderful to be able to do. I think the best~~ **One** way to keep in touch is through WhatsApp but there are lots of other ~~really good~~ options **such as** ~~and I know people who still love~~ Facebook. **[3]**
4. **[1]** for presenting a clear idea; **[1]** for using more fact than opinion; **[1]** for accurate spelling, punctuation and grammar, maximum **[3]**. **[5]**
5. Ideas might include:
   Caliban hates Prospero (his wish for bad things to happen to him, and the metaphor 'make him… a disease'); his status as a slave is shown by his unwilling gathering of the logs; he believes Prospero spies on him ('his spirits hear me') which implies he is frightened by him and this is emphasised when he mistakes Trinculo for one of Prospero's spirits and tries to hide ('I'll fall flat; / Perchance he will not mind me'); Prospero's cruel treatment of Caliban is shown in the list of verbs, 'pinch… fright… pitch'; the similes ('like apes… like hedgehogs') show how Prospero's magic spirits torment Caliban; Caliban feels this is undeserved ('for every trifle they set upon me').
   Other parts of the play that could be explored:
   Caliban and Prospero's first scene together in Iii showing that Prospero keeps him as a 'slave' and threatens him if he disobeys ('I'll rack thee with old cramps'), Caliban hates him 'a southwest blow on ye / And blister you all over', Caliban's belief that 'this island's mine' and Prospero has taken it from him, Caliban and Prospero once had a good relationship with Caliban showing him the island and Prospero trying to educate him, and Prospero's dislike arising from Caliban's attempt to rape Miranda ('Thou did prevent me, I had peopled else / The isle with Calibans'); Caliban plotting with Trinculo and Stephano in IIIii to kill Prospero and reclaim the island; Prospero knowing Caliban's plans and punishing him for them in IVi; the suggestion in Vi that Caliban regrets his behaviour and seeks Prospero's forgiveness ('seek for grace'). **[20]**

6. Ideas might include:
   Although friends (Hermia calls her 'fair Helena'), Demetrius's love for Hermia has created conflict between the two and caused Helena frustration (her repetition of Hermia's words in 'Call you me fair? […] Demetrius loves your fair'); Helena is clearly jealous of Hermia's appearance (the metaphorical descriptions of her eyes and voice being attractive) and unhappily wishes she could be equally attractive (the metaphor 'Sickness is catching: O were favour so' and the repetition of 'my'/'your'); Hermia wants Helena to be happy and tries to reassure her that she isn't interested in Demetrius ('I frown on him, yet he loves me still') but the irony of the situation annoys Helena and makes her more upset ('O that your frowns would teach my smiles such skill!').
   Other parts of the play that could be explored:
   Helena's willingness in Iii to betray Hermia in her desperation to gain Demetrius's love ('I will tell him of fair Hermia's flight'); Helena's jealousy of Hermia also causes her low self-esteem, 'For she hath blessed and attractive eyes […] I am as ugly as a bear'; Helena's jealousy also causes paranoia or anger in IIIii when she believes Hermia has encouraged Lysander and Demetrius to pretend to love her ('To fashion this false sport in spite of me. / Injurious Hermia!'); IIIii also describes how they have been close friends since childhood but their jealousy over the two men makes them insult and fight each other ('You canker-blossom […] my nails can reach unto thine eyes'); by the end of the play, they are friends again. **[20]**
7. a) Yazo **[1]**
   b) T.C.Eric **[1]**
   c) the Dancing Duggans **[1]**
   d) Nelson Jackson **[1]**
8. a) and d) **[2]**
9. The article begins by describing the theatre and making a general statement about the evening's entertainment before moving on to describe and evaluate the main 'turns', giving less detail about each one as the review progresses. The final sentence includes three turns which the writer does not think would be of as much interest and so are not described in detail. **[4]**
10. To inform readers about the theatre and the show **[1]**, and to evaluate them for the readers so they can decide whether or not to go. **[1]**
11. An example of a reasonable answer is:
    The writer thinks that the theatre's manger has done a good job in presenting 'such a good array' of acts, which he/she thinks are 'excellent'. The writer then runs through the acts and praises most of them, finding both the revue and the pianist funny. The pianist and the ventriloquist are both clever. He/she also describes and praises a double act and a violinist, before running through the remaining acts, which he/she probably did not enjoy as much. **[4]**
12. **[1]** for each idea, maximum **[4]**. Ideas might include:
    • The use of superlatives to give a positive impression of the theatre: 'latest'; 'most cosy'.
    • Flattery of the manager, who is formally described as 'Mr. H. M. Moore', in polite formal language using the passive voice: 'is to be complimented'.
    • The use of the third person to give authority to the writer's view, i.e. not saying 'I thought' but 'is already popular', 'was as amusing' etc.
    • use of adjectives and adverbs to give a favourable impression of the acts: 'mirth-provoking'; 'amusing and smart'; 'most beautifully.'
    • The use of each act's name with a clear reference to the contents of the act, e.g. 'Nelson Jackson…at the piano' so readers are informed about what they might see.
    • One complex sentence used to describe each of the first five acts, in contrast with the unembellished list of the final three acts in a simple sentence.
13. Mark against Assessment Table 1 given on p102 to assess how well you have answered the question. **[30]**

14. Ideas might include:
Romantic love is presented as something spiritual or blessed ('O heaven… bear witness'); it is infinite and more important than anything else (the pattern of three in 'Beyond all limit of what else i' the world / Do love, prize, honour you'); romantic love is full of doubts (Miranda's question and worrying she is unworthy of his love or that hers is unrequited), and can also create a happy sadness ('weep at what I am glad of'); true romantic love is presented as 'rare' but Prospero's aside also indicates that this romance has been arranged or manipulated by him; romantic love is also extreme with Shakespeare's use of hyperbole when Miranda says she will 'die' if Ferdinand does not want to marry her and will always be his 'servant' regardless of whether he loves her.
Other parts of the play that could be explored:
Romantic love coming at first sight in Iii ('nothing natural / I ever saw so noble') and being linked to magic or a spell ('they are both in either's powers'); romantic love being linked to divinity and worship ('goddess') in Iii; Prospero's wish to test romantic love in Iii and make sure it is certain ('lest too light winning / Make the prize light'); Miranda's willingness to disobey her father for romantic love in IIIi ('O my father, / I have broken your hest'); Miranda's wish to serve Ferdinand ('I'll bear your logs') and his desire to be honourable ('I had rather crack my sinews'), and Prospero comparing love to an illness ('thou art infected'); the importance of marriage in IVi to seal romantic love ('full and holy rite be ministered'); romantic love acts as a source of harmony and forgiveness in Vi where it is shown to be part of Prospero's plan to make amends with Alonso (who tells Ferdinand 'I am hers', meaning he approves of the marriage and is Miranda's father-in-law). **[20]**

15. Ideas might include:
Magic is shown to have power over love, 'Will make or man or woman madly dote', but the adverb also suggests that magic can create confusion; although used for comic effect in the play, magic is cast by Oberon as a form of revenge or embarrassment (the list 'lion, bear, or wolf, or bull' of things he could make Titania fall in love with); it is also a form of control to make Titania do what he wants ('I'll make her render up her page to me'); magic gives characters special powers (such as Puck's speed and Oberon's invisibility).
Other parts of the play that could be explored:
Puck's description in IIi of how he uses magic to 'jest to Oberon' by frightening mortals; magic is linked to the ability to affect nature (the effect of Titania and Oberon's argument in IIi); Oberon's magic is well meaning as he wants to help Helena in IIi ('he shall seek thy love') and he tries to undo Puck's mistakes in IIIiii; the comedy created in IIIi and IVi through the magical transformation of Bottom and Titania's love for him ('What angel wakes me from my flowery bed?'); the idea, at the end of Act V, that the whole play is a magical dream that the audience have shared as they slept. **[20]**

16. Mark against Assessment Table 1 given on p102, to assess how well you have answered the question.

Pages 86–101 Mixed Test-Style Questions

Pages 86–88

1. Any four from: the sun; the hills; the blackbirds; the lilacs; the garden; mist; the valley. **[4]**
2. Use Assessment Table 3, given on p103, to assess how well you have answered the question.

7–8 marks: The writer uses pathetic fallacy, reflecting the mood of the narrator in his description of nature. 'The sun began to shine' suggests that his mood as well as the day is good, as the sun has connotations of happiness. The 'blackbirds' singing is a sign of spring, which signifies the rebirth of nature and is connected with hope and optimism. Dawn also symbolizes hope and new beginning and the mist rising suggests that better times may be coming with the better weather. This mood is confirmed when the narrator meets the minister. His positive reaction to him is shown by the simple adjective 'good' and the exclamation mark that follows it.

5–6 marks: The story begins with the narrator leaving his father's house 'for the last time'; which could be a sad occasion but as he leaves, 'the sun began to shine' symbolizing happiness and hope. The birds singing and the mist lifting are also symbolic of hope and a new life for the narrator. The meeting with the minister in the second paragraph confirms this as the minister is 'good' and 'kindly', two adjectives that give a positive impression.

3–4 marks: The writer uses descriptions of nature to show a positive mood. The sun shining is a sign of happiness and the dawn is a sign of new life and hope. The minster is a 'good man', which gives us hope things will turn out well.

1–2 marks: The sun is shining when he leaves the house so we think it will be a good day. Dawn also makes you think of hope. The words 'shining' and 'whistling' give a good feeling.

3. Use Assessment Table 3, given on p.103, to assess how well you have answered the question.

7–8 marks: At the beginning the narrator tells us that he is leaving his father's house 'for the last time', but does not say why, giving a sense of mystery. He immediately changes the focus to the environment. Describing his walk from the house to the manse, he focuses on nature and signs of hope. He then 'fast forwards' to the end of his journey and changes his focus to a person, Mr Campbell, showing the warm relationship between them. He uses dialogue to explore this relationship further as well as to reveal more about his own identity and situation. The writer then uses Mr Campbell's speech to introduce the subject of Davie's father and the letter he left behind, thus intriguing both narrator and reader. The extract ends effectively with a question from Davie to Mr Campbell, 'would you go?' Whether Davie goes or not will determine what happens in the rest of the novel.

5–6 marks: At the beginning we learn that the narrator is leaving his father's house making us wonder why. He immediately changes the focus to describe his walk from the house, describing what he sees and hears. He then changes his focus to Mr Campbell. In their conversation we learn more about the narrator and what has happened before the start of the novel. What Mr Campbell tells him, especially about the 'testamentary letter' adds a sense of mystery, intriguing the reader. At the end Davie asks 'would you go?' making the reader want to know what advice Mr Campbell gives and how this affects the story.

3–4 marks: At first, we are focused on a description of Davie walking from his father's house to see the minister. When he gets there they have dialogue about Davie's father, which the writer uses to create a sense of mystery. We want to know what will happen at the Shaws' house.

1–2 marks: The focus at first is on the weather but then it moves to Mr Campbell. Mr Campbell tells Davie about his father and gives him a letter.

4. Use Assessment Table 2, given on p102–103, to assess how well you have answered the question.

16–20 marks: The writer uses Mr Campbell both to give us some information about Davie and his family and to help create mystery and anticipation about what might happen to Davie. The impression he gives of Davie's father is that although he was not rich, he was well-educated. Davie refers to him as 'a poor country dominie in the forest of Ettrick', a teacher in a remote area. This means that it might be a surprise to him when Mr Campbell implies that he is connected to an important family, the 'house of Shaws'. There is an element of snobbery in Mr Campbell's evaluation of Davie's father, as he tells Davie that he was not out of place with 'the gentry' before going on to list people that he himself is connected with, clearly meant to impress Davie. He calls Davie's father a 'worthy, Christian man', implying he was honest and caring so that when he repeats what he said before his death we think that he wanted the best for his son. The instruction to take a mysterious 'testamentary letter' to people he has never met before fills Davie with excitement: 'my heart was beating hard at this great prospect'. This letter sets up the story as both he and the reader are anxious to find out what is in it and how it will affect his future. It might also make readers wonder if his father is sending him on an adventure that is as likely to turn out badly.

11–15 marks: In his conversation with Davie, Mr Campbell tells us about the narrator's family. He gives the impression of a father who cared about his son, a 'worthy Christian man', which is high praise coming from a minister. He repeats what Davie's father said to him before he died about 'the house of Shaws', where he says he comes from. Mr Campbell thinks Davie's father was well educated and came from an upper-class family. It also adds to the mystery because until now Davie knew nothing about his background, so the reader is left wondering why that is and what his father has put in 'the testamentary letter' he left with Mr Campbell. I am not sure whether I agree with Mr Campbell's opinion of Davie's father because his instructions take him away from his home and might put him in danger. Davie is nervous about what might happen because he says his 'heart was beating hard' and he 'stammered'.

6–10 marks: Mr Campbell praises Davie's father, calling him a 'worthy Christian man'. This gives the reader a good impression of him. He comes across as a father who cared about his son and wanted a good future for him, which is why he wants him to meet the Shaws. They must be an important family. We know Davie is excited and nervous because of his 'beating heart' and this makes us excited about what is in the letter too.

1–5 marks: I think Mr Campbell likes Davie's father. He calls him a 'worthy Christian man'. The writer tells us about Davie's father by Mr Campbell talking to Davie. He does not know what is in the letter which makes the reader want to find out.

Pages 89–90

1. 'skill'd to rule'; the village master'; 'A man severe'; 'stern' [4]
2. Use Assessment Table 3, given on p103, to assess how well you have answered the question.

7–8 marks: The poet chooses vocabulary that conveys the different aspects of the schoolmaster's character and the atmosphere this creates. At the start we get a sense of his strictness from the adjectives 'stern' and severe'. Goldsmith conveys the effect this has with the phrase 'boding tremblers', giving a picture of children shaking with fear. This is reflected in the hard-sounding alliteration of 'days disasters'. But the vocabulary changes as he shows another side to the character. The pupils 'laugh'd with counterfeited glee' conveys a lighter atmosphere, though the adjective 'counterfeited' undermines this a bit. They may be pretending to laugh at his jokes because they are a little scared of him. However, the caesura in line 13 makes the reader pause and reflect on the first half of the line: 'Yet he was kind'. The emphasis on this makes us think that to the poet this was the most important aspect of the schoolmaster's character.

5–6 marks: The poet uses adjectives such as 'severe' and 'stern' to convey the schoolmaster's strictness. Alliteration like 'tremblers trace' and the hard-sounding 'days disasters' give an impression of fear among the pupils. But he lightens the mood with 'glee' and jokes' to show a lighter side of the schoolmaster. There is a pause after 'Yet he was kind', making the reader stop and think about this part of his character.

3–4 marks: The writer tells us that he was 'severe' and 'stern'. This uses alliteration to show what he was like. The pupils know him well and sometimes are frightened of him. They have 'tremblers'. But he makes jokes as well and is 'kind', so they have a mixed view of him.

1–2 marks: The village schoolmaster is very strict because he is 'stern'. But he makes 'jokes as well'. The adjectives show us what he was like.

3. Use Assessment Table 3, given on p103, to assess how well you have answered the question.

7–8 marks: The poet starts as if he is taking us on a journey, showing us the 'noisy mansion' from the outside. Then we go with him into the classroom of his childhood. The next part of the poem is from the pupil's point of view and describes the schoolmaster's character and how his pupils reacted to him. At first, he seems strict and unsympathetic but as the poem moves on we see other aspects of his character through the poet's eyes: his jokes, which the pupils laugh at with 'counterfeited glee' and his kindness. This section ends with the poet reflecting that if he seemed harsh 'the love he bore for learning was at fault.' He then moves away from the school to describe the master's reputation in the community and how he was outside school: his broad knowledge, his ability to argue and his 'words of learned length' that so impressed the 'gazing rustics'. This paints a picture of a man respected by all sections of village society. The tone for most of the poem is positive and quite lively, achieved by the use of rhyming couplets and the regular iambic pentameter. The regularity of the form also gives a sense of order and calm, suiting the nostalgic tone of the poet's story. The last two lines change the tone a bit as the poet reflects sadly on how the village schoolmaster's 'fame' and 'triumph' are forgotten.

5–6 marks: The poem starts with describing the outside of the schoolmaster's 'mansion' before going in to look at his 'little school'. The poet describes a 'noisy' atmosphere but tells us about how 'severe' the master was, giving quite a negative view. The focus changes slightly to the more positive aspects of the man's character with the poet saying that any severity was due to his love of learning. Then the focus changes from his pupils to the village in general and how much the 'gazing rustics' admired him. It ends by saying that the man and his school have been forgotten. The poem is not divided into verses and has equal length lines with a regular rhyme scheme. This makes a calm tone which suits the poet telling a story about the past.

3–4 marks: At first the poet focuses on how strict and 'severe' the schoolmaster was and how the children were a bit scared of him. Then he says more positive things about how he was 'kind' and made 'jokes'. He also says what the villagers thought about him. There is only one verse and the poem rhymes making it more fun.

1–2 marks: First the poet writes about the bad aspects of the schoolmaster but then says what he likes about him. Then he talks about people in the village. It is quite easy to read because it rhymes.

4. Use Assessment Table 2, given on p102–103, to assess how well you have answered the question.

> **Example of content (a guide to the kind of answer that would gain the marks, not a complete or definitive answer)**

16–20 marks: The reader is already familiar with the character of the village schoolmaster from the first half of the poem. He is 'severe' but 'kind' and induces a mixture of fear, respect and affection from his pupils. But that is all from a pupil's point of view, Goldsmith indicating by the use of the first person that he was one of the pupils. In the second part of the poem he gives us a different view of the village schoolmaster and places him within his community. The poet suggests that the everyone in the village shared the same view as he says, 'the village all declar'd how much he knew'. This confirms that he was thought to be learned. There is a sense that some villagers might be easily impressed, as simply being able to 'write and cipher too' commanded respect in a time when many people were illiterate. However, Goldsmith goes on to give other examples of his learning, such as his ability to 'tides presage', which might impress a modern reader more. The list of his accomplishments builds a sense of the breadth of his knowledge. The reference to villagers as 'gazing rustics' suggests that their opinion is not to be taken at face value, the schoolmaster's almost mesmeric effect on them emphasized by the assonance of 'amazed…gazing…rang'd'. However, the parson, who would also be well-educated, 'own'd his skill' in argument, showing that he was respected to some extent by all classes of society. I do not get the impression that the community loved him: rather that he impressed them. There is a sense of him being a 'big fish in a small pond', who likes the 'thund'ring sound' of his own voice a little too much. Nevertheless, he is portrayed affectionately by the poet. The regularity of the metre, combined with the rhyming couplets, gives an impression of an ordered society into which the schoolmaster fitted. Although it may be an exaggeration to say the villagers loved him, they certainly appear to have shared the poet's respect for him.

11–15 marks: In the second part of the poem the poet tells us how the village schoolmaster was regarded by the village in general, not just his pupils. He says, 'the village all declar'd how much he knew', suggesting they respected him for his knowledge. I get the impression that maybe some of them were a bit over-impressed because they themselves were not well educated. They admired him because they were illiterate. The poet calls these people 'gazing rustics' which shows they may not be good judges. However, he also says the parson 'own'd his skill' in argument. The parson would also be well-educated so his judgment can be trusted. However, the poet is also critical of him, suggesting he shows off a lot with his 'words of learned length' and 'thund'ring' voice. The metaphor 'thund'ring' suggests a less lovable maybe even violent side to his character. He does not say that people loved the schoolmaster, but they do seem to have had respect for him, as he tells us how their 'wonder grew.' Overall, I think the villagers seem to have affection for him if not love and they respect him because he is different from them. They cannot understand how 'one small head could carry all he knew,' an amusing image that sums up both his learning and their inability to judge him.

6–10 marks: The poet says 'the village all declar'd how much he knew', meaning they respected him because he was educated. A lot of the villagers are 'gazing rustics', which is a bit insulting and implies they were so stupid that he seemed clever in comparison. But the parson also 'own'd his skill' and the parson would be educated himself. The poet gives a list of all the things the schoolmaster could do and it is quite impressive. The villagers seem to have liked him but the last two lines make you think they have forgotten all about him so they cannot have been that fond of him.

1–5 marks: The schoolmaster knew a lot and had 'skill' in arguing so people respected him. I think he could be annoying with his long words and loud voice but on the whole the villagers liked him.

Pages 91–93

1. A, E, F and H **[4]**
2. Use the table below to assess how well you have answered the question.

Marks	Skills	Example of content (a guide to the kind of answer that would gain the marks, not a complete or definitive answer)
7–8 marks	Your answer: • Makes perceptive inferences from both texts • Uses well-judged details from the text that relate to the question • Shows perceptive differences and similarities between the texts.	Although Source A starts off by saying he does not like cats or 'they don't like me', it turns out that his feelings are not that different from Source B's except that he has an allergy. Source A's family welcomed cats and always had them, finding them 'useful' and sometimes 'affectionate'. The family in Source B have not had a cat before the arrival of Puss, probably because of their mother's 'horror' of them. In Source A it is the writer whose reaction to the cat differs from the rest of the family whereas in Source B it is the writer's mother who has to be kept away from the cat. The cats are similar in the way they are attached to the children, though they differ in the way they show this. Source A describes Stan following the children around as if he were 'anxious not to lose us', whereas Source B tells the story of how Puss defended her against her sister.
5–6 marks	Your answer: • Makes clear inferences from both texts • Uses clear details from the text that relate to the question • Shows clear differences between the texts.	Both writers have good memories of their cats, but the writer of Source A has mixed feelings because he discovered he was allergic to Stan. He says, 'They don't like me' and he has to avoid them whereas the writer of Source A has nothing but happy memories. Source B's writer and her sisters had to hide the cat from their mother who had 'a horror of cats' but the family in Source A felt cats 'suited us'. Both writers talk about how the cats got attached to the children. Stan used to follow the children up the road and 'Puss' protects the writer from her sister. However, Featherstone does not believe the cat really cared for him while Source B's writer thinks of the cat as her 'friend'.
3–4 marks	Your answer: • Attempts some inferences from one or both texts • Uses some appropriate details from the text • Shows some differences between the texts.	In Source A the writer says that he did like his pet cats but says that 'they don't like me' and explains that he is allergic to them. The writer of Source B also loves her pet cat but she has no problems with her, although her mother has 'a horror of cats', the opposite of Source A where the rest of the family have no problem with the cat. Source B likes to be close to her cat but Source A avoids cats.
1–2 marks	Your answer: • Gives paraphrases rather than inference • Uses some simple details from one or both texts • Shows simple differences between the texts.	In Source A the writer doesn't get on with cats and is 'allergic', Source B is different because she loves her cat who is her 'friend'.

3. Use the table below to assess how well you have answered the question.

Marks	Skills	Example of content (a guide to the kind of answer that would gain the marks, not a complete or definitive answer)
10–12 marks	Your answer: • Analyses the effects of the writer's choice of language • Selects a range of judicious detail from the text • Makes sophisticated and accurate use of subject terminology.	The language of the last two paragraphs is hyperbolic as the writer describes a conflict with her sister. The adverbs 'flatly and decidedly' coupled with the verb 'refused' suggest that she is aware of her own stubbornness being the cause of the conflict. 'War was declared' uses the imagery of serious conflict to exaggerate an everyday argument in a way that amuses the reader. The writer's 'screaming' and the use of the verb 'seize' continue the hyperbole. She uses the language of comic books or the movies when she says Puss 'with one bound flew', making the cat sound like a superhero rescuing her from a villain. She also compares the cat to a 'tigress' implying she is more like a wild animal than a pet and suggesting that her attitude to the writer is like that of a tigress protecting her cubs. In the last paragraph she changes the tone, reflecting how gentle Puss can be, which is conveyed by the onomatopoeia of 'purr' and the gentle alliteration of 'rubbed...round.'

Marks	Skills	Example of content (a guide to the kind of answer that would gain the marks, not a complete or definitive answer)
7–9 marks	Your answer: • Explains clearly the effects of the writer's choices of language • Selects a range of relevant details from the text • Makes clear, relevant use of subject terminology.	The writer uses very violent language to describe what happens with her sister. She says that 'war was declared', referring to what happens at the start of a war. This makes her sister the enemy as she is 'screaming' as if she is actually being hurt. The language is quite exaggerated. She then uses equally violent language to describe the cat's reaction, comparing her to a 'tigress', which is wild but protects its young. The language changes when she speaks to the cat and she is gentle again. 'Subdued' makes you think of the end of a war. The 'purr' is onomatopoeia to show how gentle the cat now was.
4–6 marks	Your answer: • Attempts to comment on the effect of language • Selects some appropriate details from the text • Makes some use of subject terminology.	The writer uses the metaphor of war, 'war was declared' to show how bad her relationship with her sister was. This makes us think they are going to have a big fight. She compares the cat to a 'tigress' and she sounds very fierce but when she is with the writer she has a 'soft purr' and is quite different.
1–3 marks	Your answer: • Makes one or two simple comments about language • Selects simple references to the text • Makes some simple use of subject terminology.	She uses language to say how she liked the cat more than her sister. She compares the cat to a 'tigress' which is very fierce when it attacks her sister. It is a simile.

4. Use the table below to assess how well you have answered the question.

Marks	Skills	Example of content (a guide to the kind of answer that would gain the marks, not a complete or definitive answer)
13–16 marks	Your answer: • Analyses the writers' methods • Selects a range of judicious detail from both texts • Shows a detailed and perceptive understanding of different ideas and perspectives.	The two writers' perspectives are subtly different, although both use anecdotes from their childhood to illustrate their feelings about cats. Featherstone has mixed feelings and creates humour from these feelings by seeming to worry about the reaction of 'cat lovers' to what he is about to write, hoping they will not send 'abusive messages'. It turns out that, far from hating cats, he always liked them until he discovered he was allergic to them, though he continues the light-hearted, conversational tone when he describes his symptoms: 'You name it, I had it.' Source B's author does not have mixed feelings. Her experience of cats is different from Source A's, as she never had a cat until 'a poor miserable-looking creature' arrived at her home. With her mother having a 'horror of cats' the cat becomes almost a secret and is more valued by the writer and her sisters, whereas in Source A the cats are taken for granted and valued because they 'made themselves useful'. The anecdotes display different attitudes. Source A has an ironic tone, with the writer making Stan sound slightly ridiculous, starting with the revelation that he was named after the butcher, calling him unflatteringly 'a huge ginger creature' and painting a comic picture of him jumping over fences in a bid not to be 'uncool'. Source B, although also creating some humour through hyperbole, has an almost passionate relationship with her cat. She uses her anecdote to demonstrate that the cat has a fierce protective loyalty to her, reacting 'like a tigress' to the writer's sister. To the writer this shows her 'fidelity and sagacity', noble qualities that make her at least as good as a dog. Source A too, prefers cats to dogs but his opinion of cats, even without his allergy, is more cynical and he finds them funny, enjoying watching them 'make fools of themselves'.
9–12 marks	Your answer: • Explains the writers' methods clearly • Selects a range of relevant details from both texts • Shows a clear understanding of different ideas and perspectives.	Both writers tell stories to show their feelings about cats. Source A has mixed feeling. He humorously talks about offending 'cat lovers' who might send 'abusive messages'. He then says he liked cats until he discovered he was allergic to them. He describes this like everything else in a chatty way: 'You name it, I had it.' Source B's author feels very passionately about her cat. Unlike Source A she had never had a cat until the 'miserable-looking creature' arrived at her home. This might make her more emotional to the cat especially because she has to hide it from her mother. Source A has a more humorous tone. The writer is quite unflattering to Stan, who he calls 'a huge ginger creature' and makes him sound silly as he jumps over the hedges. Source B, on the other hand is more serious about her feelings for the cat. Her story shows that the cat loves her acting 'like a tigress' to the writer's sister. This shows her 'fidelity and sagacity'. The writer thinks her cat is as good as a dog.

		Source A and his family also prefer cats to dogs but he finds them funny and likes watching videos where they 'make fools of themselves.'
5–8 marks	Your answer: • Attempts to comment on the writers' methods • Selects some appropriate details from one or both texts • Shows some understanding of different ideas and perspectives.	Source A has mixed feelings about cats. He says he liked them as a child and they 'suited' him. He is not very enthusiastic about them but he tells a funny story about Stan to show he did like them. But now he only likes them 'from a distance'. The Source B writer is much more emotional and tells a story about when her cat rescued her from her sister.
1–3 marks	Your answer: • Makes one or two simple comments on the writers' methods • Selects simple references to the texts • Shows simple awareness of ideas and/or perspectives.	The writer in Source A thinks cats don't like him. He used to like them but now he does not. Source B likes cats and thinks her cat likes her because she is her 'friend'. She uses a story to show how close they are.

Pages 94–97

Writing tasks 1–6: Use the Assessment Table 1, given on p102 to assess how well you have answered the questions.

Pages 98–101

Use Assessment Table 1, given on p102, plus the following content suggestions, to assess how well you have answered the questions.

Page 98

Ideas might include:
Helena's unrequited love, for example in her simile 'my heart is true as steel'; recurring images of her being unable to resist him ('you draw me'); she will do anything for Demetrius, including betraying her friend ('thou told'st me') and demeaning herself through the 'spaniel' metaphor and the contrasting verbs of 'beat' and 'fawn'.
Demetrius irritation with Helena's unwanted love, shown through his imperatives 'pursue me not... get thee gone' and his rhetorical questions 'Do I entice you?'

Other parts of the play that could be explored:
Lysander's accusation in Ii that Demetrius wooed Helena ('won her soul') and then turned his attention to Hermia instead; Demetrius falling in love with Helena through Oberon's spell ('O Helen, goddess, nymph, perfect, divine!') but Helena thinking it is a trick to make fun of her ('set against me for your merriment'); the resolution of their love in IVi, described through Demetrius's simile, 'like a sickness did I loathe this food: / But as in health, come to my natural taste'.

Page 99

Ideas might include:
The silliness of the Mechanicals' performance (such as Snout playing a Wall, Flute playing the part of Thisbe despite not wanting to and having a beard, and the deliberately poor writing 'I see a voice'); the stage audience joking about the play ('should curse again'); Bottom stepping out of character in the play and crossing boundaries of politeness by correcting Theseus ('No, in truth, sir, he should not').

Other parts of the play that could be explored:
Bottom wanting to play all of the roles in Iii ('Let me play the lion too'); the Mechanicals' rehearsal in IIIi with the characters getting their lines wrong ('Ninny's tomb') and Bottom being transformed; other ways in which magic causes confusion such as Lysander and Demetrius falling in love with Helena (Puck: 'this their jangling I esteem a sport').

Page 100

Ideas might include:
Ariel resents continually working for Prospero (the rhetorical question 'Is there more toil?') without getting his freedom ('what thou has promised'); he begs for his freedom ('I prithee' and the list that follows); Prospero becomes angry if Ariel does not remain subservient (rhetorical questions, the imperative 'no more!', and insults 'malignant thing'); he believes Ariel should show more gratitude and owes him for being saved from Sycorax, 'Dost thou forget / From what a torment I did free thee?'.

Other parts of the play that could be explored:
Ariel following Prospero's orders when turning into the harpy in IIIiii, or when tricking and punishing Caliban in IVi; Prospero praising Ariel but showing ownership of him in IIIiii ('Bravely the figure of this harpy hast thou / Performed, my Ariel') and in IVi ('This was done well, my bird'); Prospero releasing Ariel at the end of Act 5 ('Then to the elements / Be free and fare thou well').

Page 101

Ideas might include:
Magic is presented as astounding through Ariel's ability to take different forms ('I'd divide, / And burn in many places'); magic is linked to the elements ('flame... thunder-claps... bold waves') and is made to sound terrifying ('sulphurous roaring' and the reactions of the sailors) and powerful (references to classical gods); magic is presented as stronger than reality ('infect his reason') and also an illusion (Prospero clarifies that all the sailors are actually 'safe').

Other parts of the play that could be explored:
Magic is presented as a source of peace or restoration throughout the play, through Prospero's use of it to regain his Dukedom and make amends with Alonso; Prospero's questionable use of magic when he puts Miranda to sleep in Iii ('Thou art inclined to sleep... I know thou canst not choose'); magic as a source of cruelty and control in Prospero's interactions with Ariel and Caliban in Iii; magic as a means to punish people, such as terrifying Alonso, Antonio and Sebastian in IIIiii; the suggestion in Vi that magic is dangerous and best relinquished ('this rough magic I here abjure').